BYWAYS

OTHER BOOKS IN PRINT BY
JAMES LAUGHLIN

POETRY

The Owl of Minerva (Copper Canyon Press, 1987)

The Man in the Wall (New Directions, 1993)

Collected Poems, 1938–1992 (Moyer Bell, 1994)

Heart Island (Turkey Press, 1995)

Remembering William Carlos Williams (New Directions, 1995)

The Country Road (Zoland Books, 1995)

Phantoms (Aperture Books, 1995)

The Secret Room (New Directions, 1997)

Love Poems (New Directions, 1997)

Poems New and Selected (New Directions, 1998)

A Commonplace Book of Pentastichs (New Directions, 1998)

PROSE

Pound as Wuz (Graywolf Press, 1987)

Random Essays (Moyer Bell, 1989)

Random Stories (Moyer Bell, 1990)

SELECTED LETTERS SERIES
(W.W. Norton & Company)

William Carlos Williams & James Laughlin (1989)

Kenneth Rexroth & James Laughlin (1991)

Delmore Schwartz & James Laughlin (1993)

Ezra Pound & James Laughlin (1994)

Henry Miller & James Laughlin (1996)

Thomas Merton & James Laughlin (1997)

BYWAYS

A MEMOIR BY

JAMES LAUGHLIN

EDITED WITH AN INTRODUCTION
AND NOTES BY
PETER GLASSGOLD

PREFACE BY
GUY DAVENPORT

A NEW DIRECTIONS BOOK

Frontispiece: photograph of James Laughlin, 1987, by Virginia Schendler

Book design by Sylvia Frezzolini Severance
Manufactured in the United States of America
New Directions Books are printed on acid-free paper.
First published clothbound and as New Directions Paperbook 1000 in 2005
Published simultaneously in Canada by Penguin Books Canada Limited

Library of Congress Cataloging-in-Publication Data

Laughlin, James, 1914–
Byways : edited with an introduction and notes / by Peter Glassgold ;
preface by Guy Davenport.
    p. cm.
Includes bibliographical references.
ISBN 0–8112–1598–9 (alk. paper)
1. Poets–Poetry. 2. Publishers and publishing—Poetry. 3. Laughlin, James, 1914–Poetry.
I. Glassgold, Peter, 1939– II. Title.
PS3523.A8245B99 2005
811'.54—dc22
                                    2004016402

New Directions Books are published for James Laughlin
by New Directions Publishing Corporation,
80 Eighth Avenue, New York, NY 10011

CONTENTS

PREFACE

THESE FRAGMENTS of an autobiography were written at
Meadow House in Norfolk, Connecticut, between 3 a.m.
and dawn, when the cook arrived to serve James Laughlin his
breakfast of blueberry muffins and tea. He was not planning
an orderly account of his eighty years, only those memories
that came to him in his insomnia and got him out of bed and
down to his typewriter, where he measured out phrases in
the neat short lines that William Carlos Williams had shown
him how to write.

These carefully crafted lines, unornamented with rhyme
and with an intuited prosody as flexible as speech, are not
prose sliced up to look like poetry. They are in what should
be known as The American Plain Style, Protestant and guile-
less, as useful to Kenneth Rexroth and Louis Zukofsky as to
R. Buckminster Fuller, who wrote his *Untitled Epic Poem on
the History of Industrialization* in it.

When Joyce and Laughlin met in Paris, Joyce said,
"We've met before, at Clontarf." This was Joyce's acknowledgment of Laughlin's height and Scandinavian handsome-
ness. At the battle of Clontarf in 1014 the first wave of
Viking invasions was repelled by the Irish king Brian Boru,
an event alluded to on every other page of *Finnegans Wake*.
The Laughlins (a name that means "Danish pirate") were in
their deep past Scots of Scandinavian stock who had emigrated to Ireland, whether with sword in hand or their

household goods on their back it is not known. In time, they came to Pittsburgh to temper iron ore into railroad tracks and steel girders. Andrew Carnegie lived down the street, and the Mellons.

He grew up rich and Presbyterian in a smoky steel town from which Gertrude Stein's family had fled (to Oakland) and Mary Cassatt's (to Philadelphia and Paris). George Washington had begun his military career in Pittsburgh when it was a log fort besieged by French and Indians. The lace curtains had to be washed weekly, and the Sunday funny papers could not be read until Monday. The family traveled in their private Pullman. It was at summer camp in Wyoming that the pubescent Laughlin, running naked in a meadow, experienced his first (and spontaneous) emission of sperm. Fate is rarely so symbolic. Laughlin would spend his life as an ardent sensualist in fresh air, fleeing the fires and soot of Pittsburgh for a life defined by snow and clean white paper.

A solid education (New England prep school, Harvard, and erotic conquests rivaling Byron and Casanova) steered him toward imaginative writing, at a great distance from blast furnaces. Harvard for all its conservation of antique values has always been an inadvertent mother of avant-gardes. It brought over Agassiz, who gave us William James, who gave us Gertrude Stein. Its Greek department gave us Estlin Cummings. Rumors of Ezra Pound sent Laughlin to Rapallo in his sophomore year, and here Pound instructed Laughlin to found New Directions, a publishing house so inventive and daring that it brought Modernist writing to us as assiduously and triumphantly as the Museum of Modern Art brought twentieth-century painting and sculpture.

Literature and art get made anywhere at all—in Queens, New Jersey, Berlin, Copenhagen, Mississippi. They depend on entrepreneurs like Harry Kessler, Daniel Kahnweiler,

John Quinn, or James Thrall Soby to exhibit them to the world. Laughlin sought, and found. It was at tea with Edith Sitwell (coal tenders rumbling in the mines beneath her country house) that he heard the name Dylan Thomas. Eliot introduced Djuna Barnes; Pound, William Carlos Williams; Thomas Merton, Nicanor Parra; Henry Miller, Hermann Hesse. Borges had to bounce off French recognition. Laughlin also played a part in the resuscitation of Henry James, E. M. Forster, and Faulkner. Laughlin was inured to his authors "moving uptown" once he had given them their start. This happened with Nabokov, Merton, and most recently, W. G. Sebald. Even Bill Williams was enticed away (but returned).

Laughlin knew Brancusi and Gertrude Stein, Tennessee Williams and Kenneth Rexroth. By *knew*, I mean as intimate friends. He had a close and unlikely friendship with Thomas Merton.

A Balthus and a Klee hung in Meadow House. Laughlin's library was magnificent: the Greek and Latin classics (until he set fire to them with his pipe), finely printed books from small presses, and rare books of all sorts. A 1538 Latin Homer by Andreas Divus was stolen, together with the briefcase it was in, and his annotated *Cantos*, when he was at a urinal in Pennsylvania Station on his way to lecture at Yale.

A byway is a side road. A formal autobiography would have been a thoroughfare or highway. The memories that generated these "byways" did not need to be fitted into a chronology or have transitions provided for them. Laughlin wrote poems all of his life. They were his way of clarifying, evaluating, and interpreting the world as he found it. He was closer in sensibility to William Carlos Williams than to Pound. He was a domestic poet, private, personal, and con- genially modest. *Cultivated* is a word Henry James or Santayana might have used of his poems, meaning that he was a poet with a secure talent articulate enough to range from a seduction on an Italian beach to getting a vacuum-cleaner salesman's foot out of the door. When my cat Humphry died, he wrote an epitaph for him (in Latin).

Of some Chinese emperor in *The Cantos* Pound says parenthetically that he was "a literary cuss, perhaps you will look up his verses." Penelope Fitzgerald thought that a culture could be tested by its ability to produce and appreciate light verse (she was praising her uncle E. V. Knox's comic poems in *Punch*). In Laughlin we have the founder of one of the most distinguished firms in publishing history, a cultural ambassador and ski-resort manager, "the godfather of Modernism," educator and philanthropist, who also wrote poems. I like to think of him as a poet who was also a successful businessman.

GUY DAVENPORT

INTRODUCTION

Your life should resemble a description of your life.
—Adolfo Bioy Casares[1]

JAMES LAUGHLIN had an abiding fascination with doppelgängers. This is not surprising in a poet who invented his own double—one Hiram Handspring, who could write with ease the kind of long-line poetry that rarely came naturally to Laughlin himself. But even as James Laughlin he was a man of many names. In the office of New Directions, the publishing house that he founded as a young man, he was and still is known as JL, but he often signed a note to one of the staff simply J (with no period). William Carlos Williams and Kenneth Rexroth called him Jim. To Ezra Pound and Hayden Carruth he was Jas; to Delmore Schwartz, Jay; to Thomas Merton, J. (with a period). His annual anthologies, *New Directions in Prose & Poetry*, were first edited by James Laughlin IV, later by J. Laughlin. Who knows why he jettisoned the IV, but he was, as these memoirs of his show, conscious of his ancestry, and it is possible that he sensed something of a doppelgänger-like shadow cast by those other men in his family who carried his name before him.

In 1984, JL was researching doppelgängers for an essay that would be published as an afterword to a new edition of Romain Gary's novel *The Life Before Us* (1975), which was written under the pseudonym of Émile Ajar and won the Prix Goncourt.[2] On June 9, he wrote to Dr. Joanna Chapin, a psychiatrist in New York:[3]

Dear Dr. Chapin:

I hope this isn't too much of an imposition. I need some advice from an expert who understands Freud's doctrines.

What is your opinion of his text *Die Enthauptung der Doppelgaenger,* which I render *The Decapitation of the Other Self?* Is it authentic? If so, what is the message? It isn't in the G.W. [*Gesammelte Werke,* "Collected Works"], apparently because Ernest Jones said it was a fraud, a forgery done by a Viennese bookseller named Goldwasser, who sold it to Marie Bonaparte for a lot of money.

But I've been told by someone that the awful Fliess, who got his kicks cutting up ladies' noses, said he had discussed it with F., and that it was related to the abandonment of the Seduction Theory, some sort of an apology.

This is all quite beyond me. Please advise.

The way I got into this matter is as follows. A good friend is getting up a documentary on Romain Gary, and asked for some suggestions for the script. What interests me most about Gary is his otherself problem. He was a very successful novelist, but there was some sort of psychic crise. He invented another literary personality and wrote novels in a different style under another name. These books were great hits, which may have upset him. I believe there was some sort of a self-exposure, and then a few years later he killed himself.

What went on in his head? That's what I want to figure out. Have you read of any other cases of this kind? Is this a conventional schizoid pattern?

Many thanks for your help,
J Laughlin

Dr. Chapin was surprised and flattered to hear from JL. She had met him the year before, in June, when she rented a summer cottage on the Laughlin property in Norfolk,

Connecticut. On their first encounter—at the local swimming place, Tobey Pond—they got to talking about Henry James. At their next meeting, JL gave her a copy of R.P. Blackmur's essays on Henry James that New Directions had just published.[4] In short, they developed an intellectual rapport. A year later, when Dr. Chapin received the letter from him concerning Freud's *Die Enthauptung der Doppelgänger* and Romain Gary, she took his questions seriously and began looking into the matter of psychological doubles. Only several weeks later, in another chance encounter at a social gathering in New York, did JL own that the idea of the vexing Freudian text was a literary joke of his own devising. Dr. Chapin took JL's prankish ingenuity in good humor. After all, he did raise some serious thoughts. Besides, he had carried off his mischief with an authority born of casual erudition, wealth, and charm, some of the happier attributes of privilege. And in fact, the life story of James Laughlin can be seen as a study of *noblesse oblige*. By now this story has been told countless times, especially the founding legend of New Directions, which I first heard in 1968, the year I began doing work, as a freelancer, for the house.

James Laughlin IV was born in 1914 into a wealthy Pittsburgh industrial family, the proprietors of Jones & Laughlin Steel. As an undergraduate at Harvard, and a would-be poet, he visited Ezra Pound in Rapallo, Italy, where the expatriate American poet ran his informal "Ezuversity." Pound's advice to young Laughlin: He should forget about writing poetry and go back to America and do something useful. Since he couldn't very well assassinate Henry Seidel Canby, the editor of the *Saturday Review of Literature* (loathed for his mediocrity by Pound and JL), he should instead finish up his studies at Harvard to please his wealthy parents and start a publishing house with his family money. Pound promised to send out the word to people he knew, and the manuscripts did in fact start coming in—from Pound himself, of course, as well as Mary Barnard, Elizabeth Bishop, Kay Boyle, E.E. Cummings, Henry Miller, Marianne Moore, Lorine Niedecker, Wallace Stevens, William Carlos Williams, and Louis Zukofsky, to name just some of those whose work appeared in the first ND "Annual." The year was 1936, and New Directions was launched—while James Laughlin was still an undergraduate at Harvard—with a stake of $100,000 from his father.

This was just the beginning, and Pound wasn't even the first of JL's, and New Directions', unofficial advisors. As Eliot Weinberger says in his essay *in memoriam* for *The Nation*, following JL's death in 1997: "Laughlin's life is a tangle of paths: His prep school classics teacher, Dudley Fitts, put him in touch with Pound, who led him to William Carlos Williams, who led him to Nathanael West. Pound led to Henry Miller who led to Hesse's *Siddhartha*, the blockbuster that supported dozens of obscure poets. Williams led to Rexroth who led to Snyder who led to Bei Dao; Dame Sitwell to Dylan Thomas; Eliot to Djuna Barnes; Tennessee Williams to Paul Bowles."[5]

There were other paths as well, leading in the States to Robert Fitzgerald, Delmore Schwartz, Kenneth Patchen, Thomas Merton; Denise Levertov, Hayden Carruth, Gregory Corso, Robert Duncan, George Oppen; Vladimir Nabokov, John Hawkes, Walter Abish, Frederick Busch, Toby Olson; Robert Creeley, H.D., Michael McClure, Jerome Rothenberg, David Antin, Allen Grossman; and abroad to Federico García Lorca, Jorge Luis Borges, Pablo Neruda, Nicanor Parra, Octavio Paz; Yukio Mishima, Osamu Dazai;

Louis-Ferdinand Céline, Jean Cocteau, Henri Michaux, Jean-Paul Sartre; Gottfried Benn, Wolfgang Borchert, Johannes Bobrowski; Ilangô Adigal, Raja Rao; Tommaso Landolfi, Eugenio Montale, Elio Vittorini.

The foregoing is just a small sampling of JL's authors. He lived to be eighty-three, and during his long lifetime New Directions quite literally changed the cultural landscape of America, revolutionizing what students and educated adults read and what writers write. For a publishing house that has rarely brought out more than thirty titles a year, the list is astonishing, and until the day he died, JL had the final say in its selection, the books collectively adding up to a personal statement. Look at the copyright page of every ND publication, and there it is, even today, as an enduring testament to his taste and persistence: "New Directions Books are published for James Laughlin by New Directions Publishing Corporation."

With the success of New Directions came the attendant kudos: induction into the Order of the French Legion of Honor; honorary degrees from Hamilton College and Cornell College (Iowa), as well as Yale, Colgate, and Dusquesne Univerities; the American Academy and Institute of Arts and Letters' Award for Distinguished Service to the Arts; PEN American Center's Publisher Citation; *Publishers Weekly*'s Carey Thomas Award; and the National Arts Club's Medal of Honor for Literature. In the mid-'50s, JL took some time away—but never off—from New Directions to run the Ford Foundation's International Publications, which published the quarterly cultural journal *Perspectives U.S.A.* in separate English, French, German, and Italian editions. If all of this were not enough, there were two parallel professional lives: one in the world of sports and leisure, as the owner and developer of the famed Alta ski lifts and resort in Utah; and the other, as a poet. Publisher, entrepreneur, poet—and the last of these, at least, had a doppelgänger in Hiram Handspring.

While Pound discouraged JL's verse-writing, W.C. Williams did not. With Williams' help, JL devised his signature short-line "typewriter metrics," in which the lines in any given stanza cannot very in length by more than one typewritten character. Here is one poem, characteristically modest and classical in proportion, that appeared on the flyleaf of *Some Natural Things* (1945), JL's very first and very small collection of forty-eight pages:[6]

THE POET TO THE READER

These poems are not I
hope what anyone ex-

pects and yet reader
I hope that when you

read them you will say
I've felt that too but

it was such a natural
thing it was too plain

to see until you saw
it for me in your poem.

Throughout most of his writing life, JL in his poetry remained controlled and elegant, even reticent. And then in the mid-'70s, not long after Pound's death, there was a steady opening up in form and a growing volume of finished work, followed in the '80s and '90s (and in JL's own seventies and eighties) by an extraordinary outpouring, including the long-line poems from the hand of Hiram Handspring, the putative other self, who was also something of a comedian:

from THE CARDIAC AUTOSCOPE
> [ADVERTISEMENT]
is a useful and versatile instrument for lovers
designed originally for self-examination of the eye
    or larynx,
a new attachment developed by scientists at the
    Handspring Corporation
now extends its use to ventricular investigation
with the autoscope you can study your heart
    yourself right at home at one tenth the cost
    of a hospital angiogram
find out what your heart is like
  … .[7]

JL's *Collected Poems*, published in 1994, is over five hundred pages long, and all but ninety of them are of his later work. A revised, posthumous *Collected* would require another five hundred pages, and that's excluding the present volume. It was on JL's merits as a poet, and not as a publisher, that he was elected a member of the American Academy of Arts and Letters in 1996—a matter of special satisfaction to him.

To the description of JL's charmed public life, one might add that he was tall, good-looking and athletic as a young man, intelligent, sophisticated, well connected, literate in Latin, conversant in French, Italian, and German, and that he used his gifts to his own and ultimately to our own advantage. His gracious manner made you want to assist in his enterprise, whatever it may be. Hayden Carruth got it right when he described JL's seemingly disinterested style of charity:

Usually his letters [to me] would contain requests for help of some kind, editorial advice or jacket copy for a particular book New Directions was publishing, and this was his way: he never expressed concern for another directly—or if he did it was merely pro forma—but always indirectly and usually in terms of some objectifiable need of his own. I learned in time that this was the characteristic mode of all his hundreds of benefactions. When he paid Kenneth Rexroth's rent or bailed Gregory Corso out of the pokey, he did it impersonally, through some third person or some established agency. He didn't want to talk about it, or even to acknowledge what he had done.[8]

This gentlemanliness of JL's is in accord with his *Who's Who* biography, but how far in fact can a description of a life truly resemble that life? JL carried his share of human unhappiness, even if he was by his own comfortable admission a happy, latter-day Don Juan. Manic-depression in his family ruined his father, the generous man who had bankrolled the startup of New Directions. It drove one of his sons, Robert, to an early suicide and nearly destroyed JL as well. His first marriage, to Margaret Keyser, ended in divorce; his second, to Ann Resor, with her untimely death; his third, to Gertrude Huston, with his own. Pound's low estimation of his poetry wounded him deeply. Some of his authors, among them those he tried most to help, such as Kenneth Rexroth, could prove thankless and cruel. JL could give back in kind. He could be aloof, imperious, as well as elusive, able to close off a discussion with an abrupt but slight turn of his head. Yet it is with self-incrimination and regret that he describes in his memoirs his painful ten-year break with William Carlos Williams. Moreover, his self-confidence was often shaky. I once saw him trembling in anticipation of giving a reading at the Poetry Project at St. Mark's, in New York's East Village. He told me, "I've never read to such a sophisticated audience before." On another occasion, at an awards dinner of the

Poetry Society of America, when his hands shook as he tried to speak and he had to cut his talk short, it wasn't simply his lithium medication at work. Another side to what Hayden Carruth wrote about JL's manifold benefactions is that when he found something worthwhile for you to do that was also useful to himself, it might well concern a matter in which he believed he was incompetent—rightly or wrongly—and for which he felt he truly needed help. And more often than not you gave it, not only because of who and what he was, but because somehow you felt he needed it too.

Over the years, JL entertained many proposals for books about his life and the history of New Directions. I recall hearing about contracts for at least four of them, two of biography and two for his memoirs, but he got out of them in one way or another after having second thoughts. I remember him quoting Pound to the effect that if all you've got left to write about was yourself, then your life might just as well be over. Yet JL's diffidence wasn't total. From the start he wrote poems about his boyhood and family in Pittsburgh and about his children. Later, there were poems about New Directions authors, such as Rexroth, Nabokov, and Dylan Thomas, and about the terrible self-inflicted death of his son Robert. A series of lectures at Brown University led in 1987 to his booklength memoir of Pound, while his collected literary essays, most of them from a personal perspective, were published fifteen years before his death.[9]

Writers will often tell you that their best ideas, after cooking somewhere at the back of their minds, will steal upon them at an odd hour and take hold. For JL, his full autobiographical impulse suddenly found voice in poetry, in a suitably fluid short-line form that he adapted from Rexroth's long narrative poem *The Dragon and the Unicorn*.[10] He called these poems collectively his *Byways*, the ambling reminiscences of an old man looking back on his long life and many loves. He began publishing segments of his autobiographical poem in 1993, ten years after he started it. Yet he felt uncertain about what he was doing and looked as always to others for encouragement and advice, and he received it, principally from Hayden Carruth, whom he thanked in print for his "editorial collaboration" (see below, page 315).

In these first versions he followed his various "Byways" with what he called "classical correlatives," passages drawn from Greek and Latin history, myth, poetry, and philosophy that found resonance in his recollections. Their purposes, he wrote, were two: "First is to show the persistence of classical literature into the present. The second is to show how age-old themes and relationships are sometimes repeated today."[11] Here are a few of the correlatives he drew up in a list dated February 5, 1993, noting that "The order of the segments has not been established yet": Merton would correlate with Chuang Tzu (not, of course, Greek or Latin); the poem "The Ancestors" (page 9), with Livy's *Ab urbe condita*; his wife Ann and his son Robert, with "Demeter as the grieving mother, from *Homeric Hymns*"; his wife Gertrude (called "Ariadne"), with the "Story of Baucis & Philemon from Ovid." JL abandoned the scheme a couple of years later. Only two of these four segments were written, while none of these particular correlatives ever were. Those correlatives that JL did complete were dropped from the short "Byways" sections in his last published collections of poems. Nor in the end did he establish an order for the segments. In fact, he left no coherent manuscript of *Byways*. There were tearsheets of the published segments and a long, handwritten prose recollection of his Harvard years, the basis for most of "Harvard—Boston—Rapallo" (page 29). There was the small book *Remembering*

William Carlos Williams, the most fully realized of his *Byways*, which ND published in 1995. And there were piles of unpublished segments, some still in their earliest drafts, others in various stages of polishing and subsequent retyping by JL's secretary at his home in Norfolk, Connecticut, along with some barely decipherable fragments—these last, devastating testimony of his deteriorating condition after a series of small strokes:

```
Life at 22Øi Peerkind Str et,

st Storey's antique m ansion

on a knolll overbookind Jaɔaica

Poond in Brookljnr was a ball

of monkeys herthe inhabit natsa
```

The fragment goes on for another one hundred and thirty-three lines. JL had told me over the telephone, "Something's busted in my head," but until I saw these pages years later, typed so laboriously on his manual typewriter, I didn't understand.

A casual reader may open the present volume at any point, but an editor has to establish some form of coherence. To create order out of such a jumble of manuscript materials felt very much like trying to make a description of a life resemble that life. My inclination was to arrange the segments into a loose semblance of chronology, from the perspective of JL, the "old man" of the "Prologue," reviewing his past. This took some juggling here and there, especially in the very long segment "Harvard—Boston—Rapallo," where I filled gaps in JL's original narrative with smaller segments that, chronologically or thematically, fell naturally into the narrative. In this segment, too, I added several section titles as helps for the reader, reminding myself that, in my own experience as his editor on several books, JL was a writer who was easy to work with, open most especially to changes that would improve clarity and correct factual errors. All such emendations are noted in the endnote annotations. What I did not do, however, was create transitions or delete repetitive passages; an editor must stop at the point where his pencilings become authorial, even—or perhaps especially—when there is no author to consult. I would have liked to have been able to ask JL why he reckoned his transcription of Thomas Jefferson's 1785 letter to his nephew Peter Carr as one of his own "Byways." Was this poem to be the start of a new sort of correlative? It comes at the end of the present *Byways*, an epilogue fallen out of chronology, except for the fact that it is the last poem that JL completed for the unfinished book of his complex life that, we now know, he postponed too long.

PETER GLASSGOLD

1 Adolfo Bioy Casares, *Selected Stories*, translated by Suzanne Jill Levine (New York: New Directions, 1994), p. 1.

2 Romain Gary, *The Life Before Us*, translated by Ralph Manheim (New York: New Directions, 1986).

3 My thanks to Dr. Joanna Chapin for sharing her memories and providing the text of JL's letter to her of June 9, 1984.—PG

4 R.P. Blackmur, *Studies in Henry James*, edited by Veronica Makowsky (New York: New Directions, 1983).

5 Eliot Weinbger, "James Laughlin," in *Karmic Traces* (New York: New Directions, 2000), p. 114; originally published in *The Nation*, December 15, 1997.

6 James Laughlin, *Some Natural Things* (Norfolk, CT: New Directions, 1945).

7 *The Collected Poems of James Laughlin* (Wakefield, RI: Moyer Bell, 1994), p. 294.

8 Hayden Carruth, *Beside the Shadblow Tree: A Memoir of James Laughlin* (Port Townsend, WA: Copper Canyon Press, 1999), p. 18.

9 James Laughlin, *Pound as Wuz: Essays and Lectures on Ezra Pound* (Saint Paul, MN: Graywolf Press, 1987) and *Random Essays* (Mt. Kisco, NY: Moyer Bell, 1989).

10 Kenneth Rexroth, *The Dragon and the Unicorn* (New York: New Directions, 1952); reprinted in *The Collected Longer Poems of Kenneth Rexroth* (ND, 1968).

11 James Laughlin, "Byways," *Ambit* 131, 1993.

BYWAYS

PROLOGUE—THE NORFOLK
SANTA—DAWN

Often now as an old man
Who sleeps only four hours a night,
I wake before dawn, dress and go down
To my study to start typing:
Poems, letters, more pages
In the book of recollections.
Anything to get words flowing,
To get them out of my head
Where they're pressing so hard
For release it's like a kind
Of pain. My study window
Faces east, out over the meadow,
And I see this morning
That the sheep have scattered
On the hillside, their white shapes
Making the pattern of the stars
In Canis Major, the constellation
Around Sirius, the Dog Star,
Whom my father used to point
Out to us, calling it
For some reason I forget
Little Dog Peppermint.

What is this line I'm writing?
I never could scan in school.
It's certainly not an Alcaic.
Nor a Sapphic. Perhaps it's
The short line Rexroth used
In *The Dragon and the Unicorn*,

Tossed to me from wherever
He is by the Cranky Old Bear
(but I loved him). It's really
Just a prose cadence, broken
As I breathe while putting
My thoughts into words;
Mostly they are stored-up
Memories — *dove sta memoria.*
Which one of the old Italians
Wrote that? Dante or Cavalcanti?
Five years ago I'd have had
The name on the tip of my tongue
But no longer. In India
They call a storeroom a *godown,*
But there's no inventory
For my godown. I can't keep
Track of what's in there.
All those people in books
From Krishna & the characters
In the *Greek Anthology*
Up to the latest nonsense
Of the Deconstructionists,
Floating around in my brain,
A sort of "continuous present"
As Gertrude Stein called it;
The world in my head
Confusing me about the messy
World I have to live in.
Better the drunken gods of Greece
Than a life ordained by computers.

My work table faces east;
I watch for the coming
Of the dawnlight, raising

My eyes occasionally from
The typing to rest them.
There is always a little ritual,
A moment's supplication
To Apollo, god of the lyre;
Asking he keep an eye on me
That I commit no great stupidity.
Phoebus Apollo, called also
Smintheus the mousekiller
For the protection he gives
The grain of the farmers. My
Dawns don't come up like thunder
Though I have been to Mandalay
That year when I worked in Burma.
Those gentle, tender people
Puzzled by modern life;
The men, the warriors, were lazy,
It was the women who hustled,
Matriarchs running the businesses.
And the girls bound their chests
So their breasts wouldn't grow;
Who started that, and why?
My dawns come up circumspectly,
Quietly with no great fuss.
Night was and in ten minutes
Day is, unless of course
It's raining hard. Then comes
My first breakfast. I can't cook
So it's only tea, puffed wheat and
Pepperidge Farm biscuits.
Then a cigar. Dr. Luchs
Warned me the cigars
Would kill me years ago
But I'm still here today.

Ne quid nimis, wrote Terence
In the *Andria,* moderation
In all things. So I hold
It down to three a day:
One after breakfast, one
After lunch and one after
Dinner. A Bolivar is both
Stimulation and consolation.
They claim that what
Makes a Havana so mellow
Is the spit of the Cubans
Who lick as they roll them.
But the best leaf for wrappers
Is grown right here in the
Connecticut River Valley.

◆

Yes, we have our wonders,
Our natural phenomena,
As witness the little man
In the Santa Claus suit
Right here in South Norfolk,
This when I first came
To live here back in 1930.
I forget his real name,
We just called him
The Santa Claus man.
Even in the heat of August
He'd put on his red outfit
And his white whiskers
And walk up to the green
From his shack in the woods
Where he lived on relief

To ask at the post office
For mail from the North Pole
But of course there never was any.
Everybody loved him,
Especially the children.
He'd get a bag of penny candies
(there were penny candies
in those days, they didn't cost
a nickel as they do now)
Handing them out to the kids
Who trooped after him singing
As if he were the Pied Piper
Of Hamelin and like Mr. Finney's
Turnip that grew behind the barn
And it grew and it grew
And it never did no harm.
Mr. Santa Claus did no harm
He was our local hero.

People came from other towns
To see and talk to him.
He was written up all over
The state…then suddenly
He stopped coming to see us.
They found him dead
With his head bashed in.
The state police went through
Their usual useless motions
But found no clue who'd done it.
We buried him in the woods
Near his shack, which had
To be burned down, it was
So filthy, he had never disposed
Of his garbage all those years.

Whom the gods would destroy
They first make mad
And whom they most love
They rob of their reason,
Be it Oedipus who killed
His dad and slept with his mum
Or our beloved Santa Claus,
Now nearly forgotten.
Nobody believes me
When I tell his story;
But I have the news clips.
Does he sit up there now
On Olympus, another Ganymede,
Kidnapped like Ganymede
By the eagle of Zeus,
A cupbearer pouring out
The nectar for those
Drunken clots, the gods?
Who in the end will arise
From chaos to punish
And destroy them all?

•

And speaking of those
With whose destruction
The gods amused themselves
Notable was Dawn of Santo, Texas,
The most perfect face and body
That my eyes ever beheld,
Each part was sheer perfection,
Modeled on the Venus of Milo
And perhaps, who knows for no one
Ever saw her, the Kyprian herself,

She violet-eyed, born of the seafoam.
Dawn's father began tampering with her
When she was ten; she was placed
In a home where there were
Brutish boys and little education.
Escaping at fifteen she reached Tulsa,
Got a job in a topless bar,
Met men, too many men
Who could see only the body,
Not the person inside it.
At last came one who was decent,
A man from New York
Who treated her kindly,
Showed her respect, a good man.
He took her to New York,
Set her up in an apartment,
Sent her to high school,
Got books for her to read,
Bolstered her confidence,
Taught her how to dress.

But the cruel gods, bent on her
Destruction, caused him to die.
Back to the start, to despair,
Again the slave of her body.
When I met Dawn she was
Damaged goods. She cursed me
As I talked kindly to her,
Saying I was like the rest.
But I persisted. If it wasn't
Love it was an obsession.
In the end I know I gave her
Some happiness, some release
From her bondage, when we were

In Italy and Spain together.
One night in Milan when we
Were walking back to the hotel
From a restaurant she began
To cry in the street, at first
Softly and then violently.
She told me I had changed her.
That night she was indeed
A changed person, tender and
Passionate. We were happy
In Rome and Barcelona.
But I had not reckoned
On the spite of the gods.
They were jealous that I'd claimed
One they thought was their own.
In Burgos, cruel Burgos,
She suddenly became hostile
And silent, then catatonic.
I put her in the hospital
But their drugs didn't help her.
She escaped from the hospital
And threw herself under a tram.

I buried her in the cemetery
Of the Campo Sagrado, a long
Way from Santo, Texas. When I
Went through her suitcase
I found she had been writing
Little poems. Strange poems
That made no sense but they had,
In some of the phrases,
A kind of surrealist beauty.

THE ANCESTORS

And when we finally
Made it to Portaferry
Looking for ancestral graves,
Portaferry in County Down,
That is, an hour's drive south
Of Belfast, there was no trace
Left of the old hovel and
Potato patch, which they sold
In 1824 to take ship from Cobb
For Baltimore and the new life,
The two brothers, Alexander and
James, and the ailing old dad
Who was also James. No sign
Surviving as the parish church,
The fit little mayor told us,
Had burned with all the records
In '78. A pretty spot Portaferry
With a fine view out over
Strangford Lough, which the Danes
Called *Strangfjord* when they raided
There God knows when; and Joyce
Had told me my name meant Danish
Pirate and that we had last met on
The battlefield of Clontarf,
Cluain Tarbh on Good Friday 1014.

Disappeared without trace as if
They had never existed. The farms
And fields bulldozed, along with
The stone walls and hedgerows,

To make way for condominia
For vacation homes for Germans.
Fat Germans hiking around in
Lederhosen and Tyrolean hats.
So with the money from selling the
Place the brothers bought crockery
And a horse and wagon in Baltimore.
Heading west they sold the stuff
To the farmers in Pennsylvania.
There was enough to start a store
In Pittsburgh. It prospered and then
There was a bank. Then an iron foundry.
God-fearing people, Presbyterians,
Shrewd at deals, saving their money
To make more with it. Their luck was
The Civil War, selling rails
For the Northern armies as they moved
South. In the next generation
They sold pipe for the oil fields
In Texas, structural steel for
Skyscrapers, sheet for Detroit.

Five sons from James alone, five from
His son James, all working in the
Business. A Henry could draw and
Wanted to become an artist.
The old man would have none of such
Nonsense. No money in it. They built
Big houses on the hills of
Pittsburgh. God-fearing people who
Married their own kind, reproducing
Their own kind, until there was
Too much money. It spoiled most of them.
They moved east for the fancy living
In places like Long Island. They married
Rich girls from a better class.

Henry, my father, quit working
In the business at 40; he had been in
Charge of the company coal mines.
He devoted himself to golf, fishing
For trout and salmon, shooting birds
With an English shotgun; had his suits and
Shoes made in London, drove an
Hispano-Suiza; went to the races
At Auteuil and Chantilly, wearing a gray
Tailcoat and topper, as was the fashion;
Played chemin de fer in the casino
At Deauville, was often lucky at it.
Gave me a 30-foot power yacht
When I was 15, we sailed it up and down
The Florida inland waterway.
I called him "Skipper," he called me
"Mate." I loved him intensely. He gave me
The funds to start New Directions, though
He didn't understand the books I published.
His cousin, another Henry, got back to
Ireland by buying Castle Hyde. He rode
To hounds and kept fine horses,
One of which nearly killed him
By refusing a stone wall.
This Henry, the Boston one,
Once asked me, this was at lunch
At the Somerset Club when I was still
At Harvard, whether I was going to build
My life around skiing. "No sir,"
I told him, "I'm planning to be a writer."
"Not much money in that, I wish you luck."
Cousin Henry was right: no money in it
But a lot of satisfaction.

THE ICEMAN COMETH

It could have been eighty years ago,
Three quarters of a century.
I had my first two-wheeled bicycle;
It was a Driscoll Glorious, it had cost
My father twelve dollars. It was
A birthday present and for good behavior.
There were few cars in Pittsburgh in
Those days and no trucks. The iceman
Came to our house every day except Sundays
In a horse-drawn wagon that had no top;
If it rained he got wet. Woodland Road
Was steep, he had to stop to rest
His old horse halfway up. The horse's
Name was Frisky but he wasn't, nor was
The iceman, Mr. Carmichael, frisky. They
Were both old and tired. When he came
To a stop in our drive Mr. Carmichael
Pulled on a wooden brake attached to
A wheel of the wagon to keep it
From slipping. His big blocks of
Ice were packed in sawdust. He would
Hoist the blocks of ice, he said
They weighed fifty pounds, onto
A heavy pad on his shoulder for the trip
To our kitchen. Mrs. O'Brien, our cook,
Always had a glass of ginger ale
Waiting to refresh him before he went
On to the Greys next door. Sometimes
He would let me give Frisky a lump

Of sugar, for which he was so eager.
I had to be careful of his big teeth.

More than three quarters of a century.
Mr. Carmichael and the servants are
Long gone. I have to walk slowly with
A cane now, but I still see very clearly
What went on in the kitchen. But there
Is no iceman and no icebox with
Ice blocks. The ice gets made now
In the refrigerator.

MY SHOELACES

My life has been a series of untied
Shoelaces. "Tie up your laces,
Dear, before we go to Granny's,"
My mother says. "Granny doesn't
Like untidy little boys." I didn't
Do it. Granny is an old wet hen.
She spends her days lying on the
Upstairs sitting room sofa, giving
Orders to the servants, who are a
Bunch of lazy Irish, except for
Thomas the butler who sneaks me
The Sunday funny papers, which are
Forbidden at home. I read them with
Thomas in the pantry and he gives
Me ginger ale.

People always warn that I'll trip
Over my untied shoelaces and have
A bad fall. That only happened
Once. We were in New York visiting
Various relatives. I tripped and
Fell right in front of the Vanderbilt
Hotel. It was a bad one. I was cut
So deep I had to be taken to the
Hospital emergency room and have
Stitches. This made us late getting to
Aunt Patty's lunch party at the
Vanderbilt which put her in a pet.
What I did in the hotel dining room
Made her furious. It was the first
Time I had ever had an oyster. It
Tasted horrible and I spat it out
Right on the floor. Mother took
Me up to Aunt Patty's bedroom and
Gave me the hairbrush. And that
Was the end of the ten-dollar
Gold pieces that used to come from
Aunt Patty every Christmas.

I won't bore you with anymore
Shoelace stories, except for one.
We were in London on one of our
Summer trips "to acquire cultivation"
As they called it. Mother was off
In the country visiting a school
Friend, so my brother and I were
Alone with father. He said he was
Tired of the Burlington Hotel
Dining room, he would take us to
His club. That's what he called it,

"His club." It was a house in
Bulstrode Street, nothing that
Would tell you from the outside it
Was anything but some family's
House. A butler let us in and took
Us to the second floor in a small
Elevator. We were greeted in the
Sitting room by a handsome lady
Who looked somewhat like the Queen.
All dressed up. She and father
Seemed to be friends. They kissed.
We didn't sit down but the queen
Lady went out and came back with
The most beautiful girl I had
Ever seen. "This is Winifred," the
Queen said, "she'll entertain you
Young men for half an hour." Then
She and father went off somewhere.
Winifred was a princess for sure,
She was wearing a rather scanty
Dress but it was made of gold.
This was many years ago but
I can still see how lovely she was.
And she was nice. "What will it be,
Gentlemen," she asked, "chess or
Checkers?" Neither of us had ever
Heard of chess, so we said checkers.
As she was going to get the checkers
Set she noticed my untied shoelace.
"Dear me," she said, "your man doesn't
Take very good care of you, does he?"
And, if you'll believe it (I still
Can't) this gorgeous princess knelt
Right down on the floor beside me

And did up not one, but redid both
Of my laces. Then we played checkers
And the butler brought us ginger
And bitters, as he called it. I
Suppose I should have been embarrassed,
But I wasn't. I'll never forget her
Or our visit to the house in
Bulstrode Street.

MY PATERNAL
GRANDMOTHER

When Danny was alive I often
Sat with her in the living
Room after supper. She would
Be doing her embroidery and I
Would be sprawled on the big
Sofa reading Dickens or Trollope.
There was little conversation
Between us. We didn't need
To talk to keep each other
Company, the eighty-year-old
Lady and the boy just twelve.

She had always been a person of
Few words, never making much
Talk even when there were guests.
She never raised her voice. Even
With the servants, or with Heddy
And Homie, her two companions,
Her speech would be more in a
Tone of request than of command.
I remember her telling me once
That she'd said all she had to
Say, why go on talking? Her
Life had been one of the
Greatest comforts; since her
Girlhood she had wanted for
Nothing; the Pages were a
Prosperous and respected
Family in Pittsburgh. She
Had always been waited on
By devoted domestics. In
A more self-reliant woman
Her problems would have been
Taken in stride, but not by
Her. Grandfather's perplexing
Illness was simply beyond
Her comprehension. Nobody
Had ever gone potty in her
Family.

Danny really cared for Edwards,
The estate superintendant,
Much more than she did for Heddy
Or Homie or anyone else on the
Place. I loved him too, he was
My best friend. He would let me

Drive around with him when he
Was giving instructions and
Checking up on the work that
Was going on. He treated me
As if I were a grownup, even
Asking my opinion about some
Of the projects. When a big
Alligator fell into the well
Pit he brought me to see how
The men roped it and got it out;
No one wanted to kill it so it
Was taken over to the Apopka
Marsh and dumped there. And one
Day he took me over to Mt. Dora
To visit the packing house and
See how the different kinds
Of citrus fruit were scrubbed,
Graded, and boxed to go north
In refrigerated cars. But it
Was Edwards' tales of Scotland,
He had been born on a sheep
Station in the Cairngorms,
That I loved best. When 1 was
Only four my father had had
Made for me a little Scottish
costume, kilts, sporran, and
Even a little rubber dirk. It
Was my father's fantasy that
We were Scots not Irish as
Was the case. I loved to pore
Over Wyeth's illustrated books
For children on Bonnie Prince
Charlie and Robert the Bruce.
Bruce was my greatest hero.

He defeated the English at the
Battle of Bannockburn in 1314
That, for a time, won back the
Scottish throne for its rightful
Holders. Edwards knew the Burns
Poem on Bannockburn and taught
Me to sing it, which I was
Sometimes called upon to do at
Family gatherings:

Scots, wha hae wi' Wallace bled
Scots, wham Bruce has aften led,
Welcome to your gory bed,—
    Or to victorie.—

Now's the day, and now's the hour:
See the front o' battle lour,
See approach proud Edward's power
    Chains and Slaverie.—

Wha will be a traitor-knave?
Wha can fill a coward's grave?
Wha sae base as be a Slave?
    —Let him turn, and flee.—

And so on for several more
Emotion-packed stanzas. I can
Still hum the tune. The lines
I remember best are those of
The Scots grace that Edwards
Taught me:

Some hae meat and canna eat,
Some can eat but want it,

But we hae meat and we can eat
And so the Lord be thankit.

The day Danny died, she slipped
Away in her sleep, it was her
Heart the doctor said, she was
87, I went a little bit crazy.
I was 13 and there had been other
Deaths in the family but none so
Close, never with a dead body
Right in the house. The door
Of Danny's room was open. I couldn't
See her bed but already the room
Had been filled with flowers.
Household people and servants,
White and black, were coming and
Going, some weeping and others
Kneeling in prayer. I knew I
Should go in, I would have
Liked to say goodbye but I
Couldn't do it. I hadn't the
Courage. I was afraid of death.
I had been terrified of death
Since I was four, the year of
The kidnappers when every
Night I tried not to go to
Sleep, afraid that kidnappers
Would find a way to get me
Even though there was always
A watchman circling the house.
Death was in Danny's room. I
Panicked and fled outdoors. I
Went back of the house into the
Orange grove, the one where the

Water tower stood with the iron
Ladder going up its side to the
Big tank. There were sixty-four
Rungs but I'd done it often.
I don't know how long I
Sat on the platform at the
Top of the tower, starring
Out into space as I grieved
For Danny. I could hear
The servants calling for
Me to come to lunch, but
I didn't answer. Finally
David Dixon, the butler,
Thought of the tower and
Climbed it to bring me
Down. But I couldn't eat
Any lunch. No more Danny,
It was the end of my
Childhood.

ARE WE TOO OLD TO
MAKE LOVE?

Some fifty years ago, yes it was
That long, the summer when our
Families sent us to Munich to
Learn some German, and we met at
The opera in the Prinzregenten
Theater, you were wearing a blue
Dress and blue shoes with little
White bows on the toes, we had a
Few dates and liked each other
In a childish way. (I was seventeen
And you were sixteen.) We decided
It would be fun to put our bicycles
On the local train and go up to
Mittenwald in the foothills of
The alps. We rode around the
Mountain roads for several days.
It was lovely, such views of the
High peaks, except when it
Rained, but we didn't have much
Money so we would take one room,
But with two beds with those
Funny feather puffs on them
Instead of blankets. It was all
So innocent, like little children
Playing house. We never kissed
Or even held hands the whole
Time we were in the mountains.
You would undress and dress

In the inn bathroom and I would
Dress while you were out of the
Room. When we had spent all our
Money we went back to Munich.

We went to the opera a few
More times, we liked *Magic*
Flute the best; we took to
Calling each other Papagena
And Papageno and we whistled
The flute tune. We took walks
In the wooded parts of the
Englische Garten. I suppose
I could have tried to kiss
You but I never did. What was
Wrong with me anyway? Soon it
Was time to go back to the
States to get ready for college.

You were going to Vassar and I
To Harvard. They aren't far
Apart but for some reason I
Never tried to see you though
I thought of you now and then
And we sent a few postcards
Back and forth. That was fifty
Years ago. You married a man
In California and had children
And now grandchildren. With me
It's about the same except that
I've been married three times
And had more children. Fifty
Years ago. Then one day there's
A phone call from a lady in a

Neighboring town whom I know.
She says that "your old friend
Papagena from Munich is visiting
And would like to see you and
Meet your wife. Please come to
Lunch next Wednesday." The thought
Of seeing you again excited me.
What would you be like in old
Age? My friend had said on
The phone that your husband
Had died a few years ago.
What would you think of me
With my head getting bald
And my old man's fat stomach?
I imagined all sort of things
About you, how you would be
And what we might talk about.
Some of these thoughts were
Not rational. I imagined you
Were still beautiful and that
I asked you, quite seriously,
"Are we too old to make love?"

Yes, I really imagined that
Question being asked and
Speculated on how you might
Reply to it. The meeting at
My friend's house was not
Embarrassing. It all went
Quite easily. You had white
Hair now, but you were slim
And moved gracefully. You
Still had your special smile,
A kind of enigmatic smile,

That I remembered. You and
My wife got along pleasantly.
We talked a bit about Munich
Days but not as if it were
Some big deal. Mostly we
Exchanged information about
Our children and grandchildren.

You asked about what books I
Was publishing. Up to that
Point it was all very
Easy, very comfortable. But
Then something happened that
Was astounding, something that
I still can't understand or
Interpret. We were alone in
The sitting room; the others
Had gone out into the garden.
You looked at me with your
Enigmatic smile and said, with
No more emphasis than if you
Were talking about the weather,
"You know, James, there's one
Thing I've always wanted to
Ask you if I ever saw you again;
Why when we were staying at
That little inn near Mittenwald
Did you tear the wings off all
Those moths and throw them on
My pillow?"

Is it possible I could have
done such a thing?

HARVARD—BOSTON— RAPALLO

My father, my dear father
Whom I loved so much, wept
When I told him I had made
My decision to go to Harvard
Rather than to Princeton.
He was a Princeton man to
The core. All the men in
The family had gone to
Princeton as had he. His
Father had been a Trustee
Of Princeton. He had built
Laughlin Hall, one of those
Pseudo-Gothic stone buildings,
On the campus, and had donated
To the college a tract of
Farmland beyond the border
Stream for its much-needed
Expansion away from the
Town. My father never failed
To attend the annual
Commencement ceremonies,
Marching in the parade
Waving a tiger flag and
Wearing appropriate costume.
My brother had gone to
Princeton and became
An all-American soccer player.

But once my father saw that
My mind was made up and I'd
Given him my reasons: it
Must be Harvard because
Of the great Widener Library,
And the music of the Boston
Symphony, and the nearness
To good skiing in Vermont
And New Hampshire, he hid
His disappointment. He came
Up to Cambridge with me
To help me get settled.
I was going to room with
Larry Angel, a classmate at

Choate, and we were assigned
A sizable, if antiquated
Suite in Weld Hall in the
Harvard Yard. Weld was not
One of the beautiful old
Colonial buildings. It must
Have dated from the nineties,
Built massively of dark
Brick. But there was a
Sitting room with fireplace
And two small bedrooms
Adjoining.

The furniture was appalling,
Heavy fumed oak. My father
Trotted us over to an antique
Store and picked out some nice
Things: old American desks
For each of us, a cheerful
Persian rug, two comfortable
Easy chairs, and a bookcase
For each of us. He left an
Order with the shop to make
Up drapes which would match
The rug. Larry was speechless.
There had never been anything
Like this at Choate and such
Expenditures dismayed him.

Our next visit was to the
Tailoring establishment of
Mr. Lucas, a courtly English-
Man who had made clothes for
My father for many years.

He complimented me on my
Good posture and outlined
What would be needed: dress
For evening, a tuxedo
Would be adequate, three
Pairs of dark gray trousers,
Three tweed jackets (suits
Were not worn at Harvard),
And various shirts, some
Striped and others plain.
When we got to the shoes,
Mr. Lucas informed us with
A wry smile that the young
Gentlemen were wearing only
White shoes, generally very
Dirty, at Harvard. So we
Had white shoes (and mine
Were always filthy) but
My father insisted on a
Pair of English oxfords for
Off-campus trips.

That evening we taxied out
To Concord for dinner with
Cousin Henry Laughlin and
His wife Becky. What a spread!
Twenty acres of meadow, with
Horses grazing. That led up
To a splendid neocolonial
House of red brick over-
Looking the serene Concord
River. Henry was my father's
Second cousin, one of the
First in the family to

Abandon the smoke of the
Pittsburgh mills and settle
In grandeur on the Eastern
Seaboard. In old engravings
The Laughlin men have long,
Thin faces and the look of
Having swallowed sour apples.
Henry had other genes. He was
Plumpish and jolly, full of
Jokes and good stories. Becky
Was a New Englander, very
Vivacious and pretty. We
Were given pressed duck and
A magnificent soufflé. There
Is a family legend that the
Two of them were married at
Seventeen. Probably not that
Young but a nice story.

Becky told me that it would
Be hard for a boy from the
West to fit in at Harvard.
If they turn up their noses
At you just laugh and they'll
Get used to you. But one
Thing I must do for you, I'll
Get you on the dance list.
What's that, I asked her.
It's a list made up by an
Old lady of the Harvard boys
Who are wellborn enough to
Be invited to the debutante
Dances in Boston. I thanked
Her, I had heard about the

Dances. Boston society girls
Were reputed to be nonflammable
But very pretty. I blessed
My father for our visit to
Mr. Lucas and resolved to
Take some dancing lessons.
I have large flat feet.

In those days there was an
Unwritten but well observed
Caste system among the students.
Those who were wellborn and
Who had attended such elite
Prep schools as Groton, Milton,
Or Middlesex were Brahmins,
Well aware of their superiority.
There was a special caste apart
For athletes good enough to be
On college teams. Below these
Were the great unwashed. Those
Who commuted daily from Boston
Were the Sudras. Many of them
Were known colloquially as
"Greaseballs."

Larry Angel and I quickly
Caught on about the caste
System. In the suite next
To ours were two swells,
Peter Jay and Anthony Bliss.
They were lads from old and
Distinguished New York families
Who had been to school at Groton.
We tried to be friendly with our

Neighbors, but there was no response
Except obvious snubs when we passed
Them in the corridor. They never
Invited us into their digs or
Came into ours. It was awkward
Because we shared a shower. That
Was quickly solved: we took our
Showers in the morning and they
In the evenings. Both of them,
In second year, were taken into
The best club, the "Porc," short
For Porcellian. Bliss, let me
Report, had a distinguished
Career, first in one of the best
Law firms in New York and then
As an executive and patron of
The Metropolitan Opera. What
Happened to Peter Jay I know
Not.

The caste system is no longer
A feature of Harvard life,
Perhaps because students were
Recruited from the West and
Outlying provinces. The men
On the governing boards were
Determined to make Harvard a
National university not just
A haven for the privileged of
The eastern seaboard. Having
A father who had been to Harvard
No longer guaranteed admission
To the sons. A final factor
In the democratization

Has been Harvard's becoming
Coed when Radcliffe, the
Girls' college, once known
As the "Harvard annex," was
Merged into the university.
A loss has been the end,
For economic reasons, of
The tutorial system, based
On that at Oxford and Cambridge.
One of the best things for
Me when I was an undergraduate
Was the weekly hour with my
Tutor, just the two of us
Together, discussing whatever
I wanted to talk about, from
European history to Latin and
Italian literature, which
Were my fields of concentration.

Except for History I, where the
Famous "Frisky" Merriman held
Forth in the New Lecture Hall,
All of my courses in freshman
Year were small. Frisky
Was one of the giants of Harvard.
A big man with a totally bald
Head and a very loud voice, he
Strode up and down the lecture
Platform gesturing as if he
Were a Roman senator, as perhaps
He thought he was. His chef
D'oeuvre was the meeting between
Pope Gregory VII and the Emperor
Henry IV at Canossa in 1077.

Frisky played both parts, and
Superbly. Henry had been up to
Various misdeeds, and the pope
Had excommunicated him, a
Serious matter in those days.
Henry kneels before the pope
To ask forgiveness and penance.
He not only kneels but he
Grovels. And Frisky goes down
On his knees on the platform
To kiss the feet of the
Imaginary pope. Clapping breaks
Out in the student body, it
Is so dramatic and touching.
This was an annual event. The
Date of it would be announced
In the *Crimson*. Hordes of
People would stand at the
Back of the hall to witness
The scene and applaud.

For big courses, such as History I,
There were section men,
Often graduate students, with
Whom we met once a week. Mine
Was another renowned character,
P.P. Cram. He was as small as
Frisky was large. He smoked
One cigarette after another,
Though we were not supposed
To smoke. Cram was crammed
With knowledge yet he had never
Been able to get his Ph.D. so
He couldn't have tenure. But

The university kept him on
At the instructor level because
He was so popular with the boys.
I liked P.P. Cram—if only
For his sarcastic asides
About other members of the
Faculty—and wanted to
Please him. So when it
Came time for the midterm
Paper I produced what I
Thought was a very learned
Treatment of Oswald Spengler's
The Decline of the West, which
I had been reading during
The previous summer. I was
Pleased with my work and
expected an A. What I
Got from Cram was an E
With a note, "This is all
Balderdash. I want *your*
Ideas, not Spengler's."
I took up the challenge,
I admired him so much, and
The next paper, which was
All Laughlin, got a B+.

I soon learned that except
For sharp-headed men such
As Cram the faculty didn't
Really expect much of us
Freshmen. As it is in most
Universities, the brilliant
Professors, the stars, were
More interested in their

Research, in writing their
Books, than they were in the
Run-of-the-mill students.
I found that attendance
Was seldom taken in classes,
And the grades were given
By section men. I found
Myself cutting a lot of
Classes, putting the time
In my own reading. As for
Exams, which were given in
The vasty depths of Memorial
Hall, I developed a system.
I would take a handful of
Bluebooks and write in them
At high speed, my handwriting
As bad as possible. This
Discouraged the correctors
To the point that they gave
Up reading my scrawl and
Gave me a passing grade on
The assumption that if I
Wrote so much I must know
Something. I had no shame
About this. Marks meant little
To me. I was interested in
Getting other things from
Harvard, especially the
Wonderful books that I
Found in Widener Library.
I conned one of the young
Attendants into giving me
Stack privileges. I could
Wander as I wished through

Miles of bookshelves, taking
Down what looked good and
Reading it at one of the
Little desks that had daylight
At the end of a corridor.
I read in English, French,
German, Italian, Latin, and
Greek (in translation). All
These languages were mother's
Milk to me and they still
Are.

ADVOCATE

I began to "heel" the *Harvard
Advocate*, the student literary
Magazine, at the end of my
Freshman year. "Heelers" were
Young chaps who wanted to win
A place on the board by doing
Dull jobs around the office
Or running errands for the
Editors such as going out for
Beer or coffee. The office
Was then located in a very
Small, squalid little house
Which was stranded in an
Empty space back of Claverly
Hall on Mt. Auburn Street, a
Derelict of someone's dwelling
But no one knew whose. There

Were still dirty plates in
A closet and huge holes in
The carpet. Furniture was
All secondhand. Heating was
From an old cast-iron stove.
This sounds like a cheerless
Place to work but all was
Good spirits. Canned beer
Began to flow as soon as
Afternoon classes were over,
And merriment often went on
Past midnight. Of course,
Prohibition was still on, at
Least in Cambridge, but the
University didn't enforce it,
And the president of the
Advocate, James Agee, tippled
A bit. Agee was a genius
With the words as his career
Demonstrated. Jim won the
Yale Younger Poets Prize
Soon after Harvard, went
On to become a star writer
For *Time* and *Life*, won a
Pulitzer Prize for his novel
A Death in the Family,
And joined the immortals
With the book he wrote on
The poor sharecroppers in
The South, *Let Us Now Praise
Famous Men*.

Going back to the *Advocate*
Parties, there was one that
Nearly did some of us in.

One of the heelers had
A black bootlegger in the
Badlands of Somerville and
Brought us a mash that was
Vile tasting and also lethal.
Two of us were on the floor
In an hour, and the rest
Were engaged in a crazy
Argument about how Gandhi
Should be invited to Harvard
To speak. The next thing I
Knew we were out in the
Square lying on our backs
On the trolley tracks to
Block traffic. Frankie
Sweetser, who had lost his
Shirt and shoes, a mighty
Fellow of over 200 pounds,
Was orating. I distinctly
Remember that he was shouting
"*No passaran*," which I think
Means "They shall not pass" in
Spanish. Many trolley cars
Go through Harvard Square.
Soon we had half a dozen of
Them stalled in a row behind
Our recumbent bodies. The
Motormen jangled their bells,
Then climbed down along with
The passengers to investigate
And jeer at us. Student pranks
Were nothing new in Cambridge,
But this was an original one.
Next came a police car with

Flashing lights on the top.
The officers burst into laughter
When they saw what was up, or
Rather down. More wisecracks
About Harvard. Then, two at
Each end they rolled us off
The tracks and told us to be
Good. But they didn't cuff us,
They knew the limits of their
Territory. In those days there
Was a covenant between the
Cambridge constabulary and the
Harvard security force that
Only murder and mayhem were
The province of the men in
Blue. Minor indiscretions were
To be handled by Harvard and
Its deans. Finally, like a
Deus ex machina there appeared
The godlike form of Colonel
Apted. Although it was close
To 2 a.m., he was, as always,
Impeccably clad in a Harris
Tweed suit, a derby, and
Carrying a truncheonlike cane.
"You boys," he declared, "are
In for a lot of trouble but
If you cooperate, I'll see what
I can do for you with the dean.
Get in my car over there." By
This time we were sobering up
A bit and hastened to obey.
The Colonel (nobody knew in
Which war he had attained his

Rank) drove us to the Harvard
Infirmary where he ordered
The nurse on duty to lock us
Up in the bedlam ward and not
Let us out until we were sober.
The Colonel was as good as his
Word. The dean gave us a good
Dressing down about the college
Respecting the rights of the
Community, but let us off with
A stern warning. It was, shall
We say, a remarkable *Advocate*
Party. It was not repeated.

Freshmen were expected to
Do a sport three days a
Week. I had played soccer
At Le Rosey, my school in
Switzerland, so I chose that
For the fall. A mistake; the
Coach was a loud-mouthed
Bully. He hollered at me
Because I didn't like to
"Head" high balls. He said
I was a sissy and that the
Ball wouldn't mar my beauty.
Why head it if you could
Wait till the ball was
Lower and get a good kick
At it? In winter I chose
Squash. No matter where it
Went in the court I liked
To hit the ball as hard as
Possible. As the destination

Was, unintentionally, the
Behinds of my opponents
The number of those willing
To play with me diminished.
Spring was the best. I
Chose rowing. The Harvard
Boathouse is on the Charles
And it was beautiful going
Along the verdant banks of
The river and looking at
The Harvard houses as I
Sculled.

There are many good book-
Stores in Cambridge, but
My favorite was the Grolier
On Plympton Street near the
Yard where a lovable gent
Named Gordon Cairnie had
Been sitting on his sofa
Without ever getting up to
Wait on a customer since
The beginning of time. Nor
I think had he ever arranged
His books in any systematic
Way. Books were piled high
Against the walls in no
Semblance of order. But he
Knew where authors were
And he could talk about
Them with shrewd sense.
If a customer asked for
A particular book, Gordon
Would puff a bit on his pipe

And suggest a general area
In the shop where perhaps it
Might be. For ordering in
Books from the publishers he
Had infallible taste for what
Might interest the young
Literati of Harvard, and the
Faculty, too. Such a relaxed
Being. If there were a place
Free on the sagging sofa you
Could sit there for an hour
Browsing in books and chatting
With the writers who dropped
By.

•

In freshman year I made some new
And unconventional friends. There
Was Lord Melcarth. He wasn't a
Lord; he was from what was then
Called, as a French protectorate,
The Grand Liban, which is now
Lebanon. "Melcarth" was a
Character in one of the 18th-
Century Gothic novels. But
Melcarth seemed to be copying
His style from that of the
Eccentric French novelist and
Dandy of the 19th century
Barbey d'Aurevilly. Melcarth
Sported an eyeglass and a Malacca
Cane with a silver head of the
Devil. Instead of a necktie he

Wore a French cravat and favored
Velvet waistcoats of various
Colors. He described himself as
A writer but so far as I know he
Never published anything. He
Would have been a bore except
That he was very witty. Give him
A subject and he could reel off
An amusing epigram for it.

Two new friends, Joe Pulitzer
And John Cromwell, are worth
More attention. Joe's grandfather,
The newspaper publisher, was
The man honored by the Pulitzer
Prize. From him Joe was later
To inherit the *St. Louis Post-Dispatch*,
Which he published for many
Years with distinction. He also
Formed a first-rate collection
Of Impressionist paintings. Joe,
Too, was an elegant dresser, but
In conventional style. He had
A grand piano in his room and
Played it well. He drove a
Ferrari sports car, but never
Let any of us drive it. His
One affectation was a curious
Slow drawl that enhanced his
Sarcasm, which could be almost
Cruel. I remember it well
Since I was often the butt
Of it because I came from
Pittsburgh, a city with no

Culture, and because I had
Not been to St. Marks, as he
And Cromwell, his roommate,
Had been. Despite his jibes,
I liked Joe. I found his
Hauteur and his supercilious
Snobbery amusing. Often when
We talked about girls the name
Of a mysterious "Fleurie"
Would come up. Gradually, it
Came out, unbelievable as it
Seemed, that "Fleurie" was a
French girl whom Joe was
Keeping at the Boston Ritz.
I clamored to meet her but
With no success. "She wouldn't
Like a peasant" was Joe's
Excuse.

John Cromwell was quite the
Opposite of Joe, though he
Came of good family, which
Included an ambassador. He
Was shy, and diffident, not
Easy to talk to. John had
One curious tic, not more
Than that, I think. To put
It coarsely, he was in love
With his own feet. Almost
Invariably when I dropped by
The Cromwell-Pulitzer apartment,
John would be stretched out
On the lounge chair without
His socks and shoes, not

Reading, just admiring his
Own feet. He didn't do anything
To them or with them, he just
Studied them, almost as if
They weren't part of him.
Joe would say, "We're playing
The feet game," and circle one ear
With a finger. Whatever the feet
Games meant, Cromwell was thinking
When he was self-contained. It turned
Put that he was a writer, and a
Pretty good one. He published some
Stories in the *Advocate*. Later in
1942, I received in the mail a
Privately printed novel called
Egon Rendy, brought out by the "Non-
Pragmatic Press." The introduction
Begins with the statement: "I am
Publishing this book myself because
No one else likes it." Then it
Goes on to say: "The book is about
Attitudes of mind and why they are
Bad." And further on: "It is a
Destruction of self-consciousness
As a pattern of thought." About
Fifteen years later I ran into
Cromwell in Paris. He had a
Renault and was living alone in
A nicely furnished apartment.
He told me he was writing another
Book but wouldn't let me see
Any of it.

HONORA

Freshman were almost never
Invited to the Boston debutante
Dances, so unless they had
Relatives, my classmates saw
Little of the upper-crust girls.
They had to turn to the "Cliffies,"
The students at Radcliffe, whose
Campus was not far from the Yard.
For many of my friends the
Cliffies were regarded with
Scorn, even disdain. It wasn't
Very nice. The boys would go
Out with them, paw them about,
Then criticize them for not having
Style or their Middle Western
Accents. But I lucked out. I
Met Honora, who gladdened the
Winter and spring for me. She
Was from Georgia and she was
A little Georgia peach. She
Was bright, a scholarship student,
And she was pretty and shapely,
A grown child full of affection
And good spirits. Auburn hair
Down to her shoulders. Just
Enough of a drawl to prove
That she was from "Jawjia."
She lived in one of the Radcliffe
Dorms, not far from the Yard,
Where I'd pick her up. (I'd
Gotten a Ford roadster, which

Cost me all of $900. You can
Imagine what it would cost now.
I kept it in a garage on Center
Street (no overnight parking
Was allowed in Cambridge).
Honora and I took to each other
Very readily. No problem to
Find things to talk about. She
Was planning to major in art
History and I was then thinking
Of medievalism; my love of the
Classics came later. On our
First dinner date we were
Holding hands on the table by
The end of the meal. On our
Second we were kissing, long
Kisses, in the car, and so it
Went. There was never any doubt
That we really were fond of each
Other. I loved her spirit and,
Excuse the word, her sexiness.
She was a toasty little biscuit,
And it came so naturally to her;
Given the right circumstances,
It was instinctive, never put
On. Some nights after dinner we
Would drive out toward
Concord to park in a side woods
Road where we were alone to
Snuggle in the car. I never
Asked her but I think she must
Have had an experienced lover
Down in Georgia. She knew so
Much more than I did. I learned

A lot from my lovely teacher,
What would please and what would
Excite. We pleasured ourselves
Mightily, but we never "went
All the way." Her mother had made
Her promise not to "go all the
Way," and she didn't. Not that
I pressed her for that, having
In mind my father's embarrassed
Strictures about the danger of
Conception. In those days there
Were no condoms, at least in
The drugstores on the square.

One night we had a little scare
When a police car drove up
Beside us and the officer shined
His light on us, half dressed as
We were. But he was a jolly
Policeman. He just laughed and
Told us, "Have a good time
Children. Give her a squeeze
For me. And keep your lights
On when you're parked."

It all seemed to be too good to
Be true. And indeed it was.
Young as she was, she had ideas
About getting married, but I
Hadn't yet inherited and
Wouldn't have been able to
Maintain a wife. Soon she
Told me she had arranged to
Move from Radcliffe to

Mount Holyoke for her next
Year. "I love you, James,
But I can't go on with you
The way things are." It was
A tearful parting but I
Understood. I never saw
Honora again. A few years
later I learned that she
Had married a young man in
Memphis, a businessman. I
Often think of her, even
Now with a certain remembered
Longing and with gratitude
For what she gave me of
Herself. *Est amare dulce*
in juventute.

◆

In the fall of 1933 I found myself
Living rather palatially in Eliot
House. It was the custom for freshmen
To live only in the Yard and then to
Be moved on to one of the residential
Houses with which the Standard Oil
Heir Edward Harkness had endowed
The campus. Harkness's intention,
I believe, was to have these houses
Be like the individual colleges of
Oxford and Cambridge, but it didn't
Quite work that way. Classes were
Still held in the Yard to which
The students walked from their
Houses. Eliot House, built in

Colonial brick and bordering on
The Charles, was the most attractive
Of the Harkness group. I applied
To live there and was lucky to be
Accepted. And I had the luxury
Of a tutor with whom I met
Privately once every fortnight.
Robin Matthewson was a charming
Young Englishman, a don on leave
From All Souls, to see what the
States were like. After some sessions,
Robin perceived that I was not
Keen on reading scholarly books.
We devoted our time pleasantly to
My asking him questions about
European history, and his
Translating the Greek poets
For me at sight. The beauty
Of an English education, to be
Able to roll off the strophes
Without having to look up words
In the lexicon. Eliot House was
Named not for T.S. but for Charles
William, Harvard's greatest modern
President, who pioneered the elective
System and turned a college into a
University. It was so comfortable,
A style befitting young gentlemen.
Fireplaces in every sitting room,
A maid to clean and make the beds.
In the dining hall there were
maids in uniform to serve a choice
Of entrées. No drink in the hall,
But in the basement there was a

Room for beer, nothing stronger.
The high point in the hall each
Year was the performance by the
Students of an old English play.
The plays were staged on a
Platform, without scenery but
With costumes of the period.
My year it was Ben Jonson's
Comedy *Bartholomew Fair* (1614).
I was cast as Mooncalf, a tapster.
An important part. I was clad
In a red jerkin, full hose
And a velvet hat. I had all
Of ten lines to speak and put
My best into them. The climax
Of the play was when Frisky
Merriman, the master of the
House, classically garbed in
A toga, came down the aisle,
To a clamor of drums and
Cymbals, as the god Dionysius
To bless the proceedings. He
Was a popular housemaster.
There was prolonged applause.

The quality of life in the
Harkness houses depended on
One's entry mates. (The
Houses weren't designed with
Central stairwells, but with a
Series of small stairs serving
Half a dozen rooms.) On the
Third floor of E entry with
Me was MacVitty. I'd love to

Know what has happened to him.
He was planning to become an
Architect; he could draw
Anything so it looked to be
Done by a master. His one
Peculiarity was that from the
Beginning to the end of the
Year he never unpacked his
Wardrobe trunk, which stood
Open in the middle of his
Sitting room. When his clothes
Came back from the laundry
Or the cleaners he would store
Them back in that trunk instead
Of using the bedroom closets.
I ventured to ask him about
This. "It's handier," he said.
I hope he has designed some
Buildings that are in every
Way handy.

My favorite friend in our
Entry was "John the Cod,"
John Coddington, the best-
Liked man in the house. The
Cod was prematurely portly
And had bulbous eyes behind
His spectacles, but his good
Humor was perpetual and he
Kept us all laughing with
His anecdotes. "The Cod's"
Academic situation was like
That of P.P. Cram. He had
Never finished his dissertation,

But he was such a good teacher
He was kept on as an instructor.
His subject was European history,
But his passion was genealogy,
That is the genealogy of the
Royal and noble families of
Europe. He knew *Burke's Peerage*
And the *Almanach de Gotha*,
Which covers the houses
Of Europe, by heart. Toss a name
To him and he would give not
Only the lineage but round it
Out with stories about the
Role that person and his line
Played in history. I only
Caught him at a loss once when
I asked about Geneviève of
Brabant. He couldn't place
Her but when we looked her up
In the *Britannica* she turned
Out to be not a historical
Figure but the heroine of a
Medieval legend. A further
Point about Coddington which
May or may not relate to his
Love of genealogy; he kept
Four cats on which he lavished
Great affection.

Ted Spencer, professor of
English, comes later in this
Narrative but he befriended
Me that year in Eliot House.
Some of the professors had

Suites in the house and his
Was on the ground floor of
My entry. He had a piano in
His rooms and he would let
Me come to hear him play.
He could sight-read Mozart
And Bach without an error.

By nature, I guess, philosophy,
With a few exceptions such as
Plato, has always been a *terra
Incognita* for me. My language-
Oriented mind rebels against
It. From early on I took refuge
In the axiom of a German friend
That *Unsere ganze Philosophie
Ist eine Berichtigung des
Sprachgebrauchs.* ("All philosophy
Is a correction of linguistic
Usage.") But when I heard that
The great Alfred North Whitehead,
The author of *Process and
Reality,* would accept undergraduates
In his course I decided I would
Venture it. I'm glad I did.
I could seldom understand what
His lectures were about, but
They brought me into contact
With a great and lovable man.
Whitehead was a delicious, or I
Would even say an adorable man.
A little round fellow, in his
Seventies then I'd say, who
Gave the impression that we

Were worth his time no
Matter how stupid we might
Be. A wonderful smile, a
Wonderful chuckle. The course
Was given in a small lecture
Room in Emerson Hall. Whitehead
Was on a platform, sitting
In an armchair that tilted
Back. He would keep tipping
The chair backward till we
Were all convinced that he
Would fall over on his bald
Head. But he never did. At
The beginning of the course,
As if to welcome us, he said,
"You know I'm really a muddle-
Headed sort of man." And he
Proved to be a very kind one.
When our first papers came
Back there wasn't a single
One that had a mark lower
Than "A-" and some of us
Got "A+++'s." I loved his
Classes though I could grasp
Very little of what he said.
There was such a radiance, a
Love of learning, came out of
Him. Toward the end of the
Course it began to penetrate
My dumb head that Whitehead
Was creating a philosophy of
Organism which viewed the
Universe as processes of
Becoming, with God as inter-

Dependent from the world
But developing from it.

A professor who became a friend
Was "Matty" Matthiessen, famous
For his book *American Renaissance*.
He too had an office suite in Eliot
House where the door was always
Open to students. A small man
With a big heart. The attention
Which he gave his students was
Legendary. I took his course in
The history of American literature,
And he granted me many sessions in
His office. Before I signed up
For his course I was warned that
Matty was "left," perhaps even
An undercover member of the
Communist Party. Of this slander
I saw no trace at all. To be
Sure, in his lectures he had to
Deal with social influences but
He put no spin on his treatment
Of them. I had always thought
Of Herman Melville as only the
Author of *Moby-Dick*. Matty put
Me on to Melville's poetry and
Soon had me sharing his praise
For it. When, years later, I had
Started the Poets of the Year
Series at New Directions, one
Of the most applauded booklets
Was a *Selected Poems* of Melville
With Matty's introduction.

I kept in touch with Matty
After I had finished Harvard
And was deeply saddened by his
Fate in 1950. Matty was gay
But he had kept himself closely
Closeted, a necessity for a
Career at Harvard. For twenty
Years or so his companion had
Been a gifted painter. They
Shared a cottage on the Maine
Shore, where they spent weekends
And vacations. Then the friend
Died of cancer and Matty was
Unable to bear his loss. He
Rented a room in the hotel at
The North Station and threw
Himself out the window.

By sophomore year my interest
In history had declined and
Shifted to the classics. I
Read Virgil with Professor
Pease, a somber man who had
A passion for Latin. He had
Been president of Amherst,
But gave it up to return to
Harvard to teach Latin. He
Was a very moral man. To the
Amusement of the class he
Spent a full hour proving,
Word by word, that Aeneas and
Dido had done nothing improper
When they spent the night
Together after the great storm
In Book IV of the *Aeneid*.

There were student escapades
Which would have caused Pease
Great pain, had he known about
Them. One night three of us were
Down on the railroad tracks near
The Back Bay Station. We were
Shouting out "Fair Harvard."
That meant a spell in the Boston
Poky till we were rescued. Then
There was the Old Howard burlesque
House in Scollay Square. The
Dancers were not beauties, but
There was one who could do
A trick I've never seen elsewhere.
She could rotate her boobs in
Opposite directions as she danced.
This always brought down the house.

◆

Now that the class had become
Sophomores, some of us were
Invited to the Boston debutante
"Coming out" dances. These were
Very pleasant affairs, usually
Held in the ballrooms of the Ritz
Or the Somerset Hotel. If it
Was for a girl from a prosperous
Family there might be a dinner
Before the dance. The girls,
Lovely creatures in their very
Modestly cut gowns, were a
Delight to see. *Des jeunes filles*
Bien éleveés en fleur. They

Were of course well chaperoned
By mothers or aunts who were
Lined up in chairs along the
Walls. There were two rules to
Be respected: no dancing that
Was too snug, and each young
Man must dance one dance with
The bishop's daughter, who was
Nigh on seven feet tall. To cut
In was permissible. For a couple
To leave the ballroom was not
Acceptable. If a young man
Arrived tipsy he was sent away
By the head usher. If there was
A dinner the waiters were
Coached to refill a wineglass
Only once. The girls were
Taken home by their chaperones,
Not by a partner.

I enjoyed these parties very
Much. There was a refinement
Which never would have been found
In my native Pittsburgh. But there
Was one evening, it was a party
At the Somerset Hotel, when I
Had cause for alarm. Looking
Out across the ballroom I was
Astonished to discern my father,
My dear father, in full waltz
With Lolly Farley. Obviously,
He had crashed the gate. What
To do? I escorted my partner
To her mother, apologized, and

Headed across the floor. How
Would I get him out of there if
He had been drinking? But my alarm
Was needless. From where I stood
I could see that he wasn't tipsy,
That he was enjoying himself, and
That he was amusing his partners.
I decided not to go speak to him;
That would be an embarrassment.
I went back to my own dancing,
But keeping an eye on him. In
About half an hour he disappeared.
I couldn't find him anywhere in the
Hotel. Obviously he had had his fun
And returned to his apartment in
The Algonquin Club.

FATHER

When he graduated from Princeton
My father had gone to work in the
Family steel mills in Pittsburgh.
For a few years he helped with
The electrification of the big
New plant down the Ohio River at
Alequippa. He married young, my
Mother was a great beauty, and
In time there were two sons,
My brother Hugh and myself. His
Next big job was managing the
Coal mines of the company. They

Were up the Allegheny River, an
Hour's drive from Pittsburgh.
When I was small I remember his
Taking me with him up to the
Mines. For a child it was very
Exciting to watch the stream
Of coal coming out of the mine
On moving belts, go through
The washer and then be dumped
Into barges to go down the
River.

My father was not indolent, he
Had a lot of energy, but a few
Weeks after his father, my grand-
Father, died, he resigned from
The company. He had done his
Duty well but had never liked
The mills. He didn't have the
Spark in him to become a steel
Baron; and there were a number
Of cousins to replace him.
Beyond that, he had never much
Cared for the ambiance of
Pittsburgh, with its clouds
Of smoke from the mills, a
Perpetually gray atmosphere.
Nor did he like the dull
Boredom of the talk of his
Fellow members at the Duquesne
Club which centered on baseball
If it wasn't money. So, much
To the chagrin of my mother,
And of her friends, my father
Set out to remake his life.

My father loved outdoor sports.
He was a 4-handicap golfer. At
First he played the courses
Near Pittsburgh, then started
Playing the good courses in
The South, in the Carolinas
And Florida. Then, as he
Wandered further from home,
It was the great courses of
Scotland, St. Andrews and
Gleneagles. He didn't like
To play alone so he arranged
With a rising young star
Named Bob Stupple to be his
Private pro, not that he
Needed instruction but Bob
Was good company to travel
With. As I got older he would
Sometimes take me along on the
Scottish trips. What I liked
Best were the herds of sheep,
Tended by old shepherds, which
Were used to keep down the
Grass and the roughs. I spent
As much time hunting for lost
Balls as I did playing. But
I liked the putting.

My father was also a skilled
Fly caster. He tied his own
Flies and understood the
Seasons of insects on which
Trout would feed. To practice,
He would plant a cigarette

Butt in the grass, then walk
Off fifty paces and cast for
The butt. Often he would pick
It up with his hook after two
Or three casts. Don't forget
The ducks. My father was
Sharp with a shotgun (a
Double-barreled one from
London). In the fall, he
Would go to various wetland
Places where there were
Blinds in which he would
Hide till the mallards
And teal came over on
Their migratory flights.
He would keep on shooting
Till dark, drive home
With the little carcasses
Which would be hung up
In a special room in the
Basement to be "ripened"
Until they were ready
To be eaten.

There was one exception to
The rule of outdoor sports.
My father detested bridge,
Which he considered a ladies'
Game, but he loved chemin de
Fer, and he was good at it.
Thus an annual stop on his
Travels became the casino
At Deauville, a resort on
The north coast of France.

No golf course there then so
Bob Stupple was left behind.
There were rumors of a lovely
Madame de Hauteville who
Kept him company at the
Baize tables.

My mother bore my father's
Absences with Christian
Patience and without reproach.
She believed absolutely that
On her demise she would be
Transported to Heaven, where
All her woes would be washed
Away. I know that she prayed

For my father, but to no avail;
He pursued his headstrong course.
You may ask where the money came
From to support his way of life.
That's easy to answer. He had
Inherited two thirds of his
Father's estate, which was, in
Those days of low taxes, not
Inconsiderable.

I've left for the last an item
Of extravagance which affected me.
One day when I was just past
Fourteen my father suggested
That we go down to Florida.
"What's the point," I asked,
"When grandfather's place has
Been sold to the missionaries
For a boarding school?" "Trust me,"
He said, "you'll be surprised."
So we took the train and got off
At Daytona, which has a very big
Beach where the sand is so hard
That cars can race on it. Was
He going to go in for racing?
Not at all. We took a taxi to
The marina, which is not on
The ocean but on the inland
Waterway which runs down the
Whole eastern coast of Florida.
We walked out on the pier and
There amid the other boats that
Were tied up was a beautiful
Little cabin cruiser. My father

Walked up to it and told me to
Get aboard. "It's yours, Mate,
And it's named *Sarsho*, which
Means fish in Seminole language."
I burst out crying at such a gift.
It turned out that the *Sarsho* had
Been designed by my father. He
Showed me his sketches, explaining
Various points. "But there's one
Thing you must promise me. This
Is light construction. You must
Never take it out into the ocean.
Big waves might break it up." It
Wasn't a large boat, only about
Thirty feet from stem to stern,
But it had everything just right
To accommodate two people.

The Florida inland waterway
Isn't exactly beautiful. Mile
After mile, the banks are thick
Mangrove swamp, except where there
Are scattered Negro houses.
But the birdlife is wonderful,
Every kind of water bird you
Can think of. And the silence,
Pervasive silence. And the
Clouds drifting along overhead,
We had enough canned food in
The boat's fridge till we came
To the waterside town of Stuart.
The mosquitoes were bad but we
Managed to sleep when we were
Anchored along the bank at

Night. In the noon heat we'd
Anchor to skinny-dip and then
Sunbathe on the forward deck.
We'd heard tales of water
Moccasins but didn't see
Any. We spotted one alligator
But he was asleep on a palm
Log and didn't budge. My
Father was patriotic: every
Morning he'd raise an American
Flag and a Princeton flag in
The stern.

Our destination was Palm Beach.
We made it there in four days.
Suddenly at that point the
Waterway widens into a broad
Lake. The big winter houses
Of the rich people are on a
Long island on the ocean side,
While the plain houses and stores
Of ordinary people are on the
Mainland in West Palm Beach,
Reached by several causeways.
We had a good choice of
Ocean beaches on which to swim,
At houses belonging to various
Relatives. But we liked best
The magnificent pink palace of
Great-aunt Edith, daughter of
The Pittsburgh man who had
Developed the iron ore deposits
Of the Upper Peninsula of
Michigan. Aunt Edith was not

In residence, but the guardian
Showed us around the house. It
Was like a mixed-up museum.
Each of the main rooms had
Come from some building in
Europe, but the way they had
Been mixed together by the
Architect they didn't match.
The total effect was one of
Confusion. The only part I
Liked was Aunt Edith's dining
Room. It was, the guardian
Proudly told us, a refectory
From the University of Salamanca,
Built by Alfonso IX in 1230.
Marvelous carvings in the
Woodwork of devils and angels.
Aside from the swimming, we
Had some fine walks, one day
All the way you can go north
And another all the way you
Can go south on the island.
Since most of the winter
People hadn't come yet,
We were able to inspect many of
The fancy houses. Evenings
We would have dinner at one
Of the restaurants . . . and
Then it was chemin de fer
For my father. There never had
Been a casino in Palm Beach
But there was a place called
Bridges, which looked like a
Dwelling, where there was

High-stakes gambling for men
Who were known to the proprietor.
My father had brought along his
Tuxedo. He would put it on,
Then get into the dinghy which
Trailed *Sarsho* in case the
Engine went dead, and row
Himself ashore. Usually he
Was gone until midnight. I
Passed the time reading *The
Last of the Mohicans* and
Playing the Gramophone; my
Favorite record was Rudy
Vallee singing the "Stein
Song." (Does anyone remember
It now?) We had other good
Trips on *Sarsho*. One year
We went north up to Georgia
On the waterway. Another
Time my father had *Sarsho*
Trucked to New Orleans for
A voyage up the Mississippi
With stops along the way to
Visit the beautiful old
Plantation mansions.

It was all too good to be
True, our affection for each
Other and the things we did
Together. It couldn't last;
And it didn't. When he was
Fifty-three my dear father, without
Any warning, fell victim to
Manic-depressive psychosis,

Or violent mood swings as it
Is popularly called. His whole
Life pattern changed. It was
A disaster for this athletic
Man who had never been ill
To be crippled by a mental
Disease. At first he started
To drink heavily but that
Only made the cycles worse;
More abject depressions and
More frantic periods of mania.

THE AFTERMATH

My father had doted on
Automobiles all of his
Life. So when the next
Summer he invited me to
Fly to England I was hardly
Surprised to be met at
Heathrow by an elegant
Hispano-Suiza. I think
It was a phaeton town
Car, but in any case the
Driver had to have a
Raincoat because there
Was no roof over the
Driver's seat. Father's
Driver was named Plumb.
He was a most engaging

Fellow. If it wasn't
Raining I spent a lot
Of time beside him in
The car, enjoying his
Endless stories about
England and the noble
Families for whom he had
Driven. In London we
Put up at the little
Burlington Hotel which
Is at the end of the
Burlington Arcade, where
I had bought lead soldiers
Of the British regiments
When I was a child. I
Knew I was in London
When early next morning
Father came in with a
Bag of strawberries
(English strawberries are
The sweetest in the world)
That he had gotten from
A street vendor. There
Were many things to do in
London. Among the most
Important, to my father,
Was to get me measured in
Sports coat and flannels
By his tailor in Sackville
Street. I love to walk the
Streets of London; history
Is at every turn from
Buckingham Palace where
The guardsmen stand as

Motionless as statues to
Tyburn, where in olden
Times unfortunates were
Hung for stealing a sheep.
My father was not keen on
Picture galleries but I
Visited the National and
The Tate. Nor did he care
Much for ballet but that
Summer great stars such as
Danilova, Toumanova, Massine,
And Riaboushinska were dancing
At Covent Garden where I
Lured my father for several,
To me, memorable evenings.

When I sensed that he had
Had his full of culture
We headed north, with Plumb
At the wheel, for the golf
Courses of Scotland.
We played the famous St.
Andrews tournament course
Which seemed to me rather
Antiquated in its layout,
And several times at
Pitlochry and Gleneagles,
Which pleased me aesthetically
Because they made me feel
That I was walking over the
Scottish moors. There were
Sheep grazing in the roughs,
Tended by venerable shepherds,
Who looked worn but wise.

After Gleneagles we headed
South through the borderlands
To play the courses along
The edge of the Irish Sea.

Back in London and then Plumb
Put the Hispano-Suiza on the
Ferry to go with it to France.
The star of the French visit
Was a French lady in her
Early forties named Geneviève
De Hautecoeur. I don't know
How my father had met her but
It was a strong attachment.
She was from Provence but had
Had an English governess so
She spoke flawless English.
But she let me practice my
Schoolboy French by talking
Bad French to her. She was a
Lovely creature, blonde and
Beautiful and intelligent.
She could recite the poems
Of the poets of the Pléiade
By heart. I suppose there must
Have been a husband at some
Point but she never spoke of
Him. In Paris we put up at
The Hotel Pont Royal
On the Left Bank. It was
Near Geneviève's apartment
Where often my father lingered
Late. She knew all the best
Restaurants and we ate royally,

The food accompanied by my
Father's favorite vintage of
Corton. Our favorite restaurant
Was the Grand Véfours in the
Arcade of the Palais Royal,
Its decor, a painted eighteenth-
Century ceiling, as remarkable
As the food and the service;
The waiters seemed to be dancing
When they served us, and on
The back of each banquette
There was a little bronze
Plaque that gave the name
Of a famous person who once
Sat there.

Most of my time in Paris
Was spent touring the art
Museums, or scanning the
Stalls of the second-hand
Booksellers on the avenue
Beside the Seine, or exploring
Parts of the city I didn't
Know. To reach them I'd
Take the Metro to a distant
Station, and get off there to
Walk around. The names of
The streets were full of
History. One day I went out
With father and Geneviève
To the racing at Chantilly.
I saw at once that the
Spectators were more interested
In walking around below the

Grandstand, greeting each
Other and showing off
Their dressy clothes, than
They were in paying attention
To the horses. Geneviève had
An extraordinary hat for the
Races. It was like a round
Satin dish on which several
Kinds of small birds appeared
To be feeding. It was much
Admired. My father was elegant
In conventional garb: a light
Gray cutaway dress outfit
With a folded cravat and a
Gray topper to match. He
Placed a few bets but his
Luck that day was in enjoying
The company of Geneviève, as
Did I, rather than on the
Horses. She was an exquisite
Woman and she talked well.
Before we left Paris my
Father took me with him to
Cartier's to pick out a gift
For her. Such baubles. We
Looked at tray after tray
But chose for her a modest
Sapphire ring with a flawless
Stone that seemed to flash
In the sunlight.

After Paris we headed north
To Deauville on the Channel
For the beach and casino.

The Hotel de la Mer, right on
The beach, was a stuffy
Overdecorated place mostly
Full of fat bourgeois and
Their fat wives but the
Food was edible. I didn't
Accompany my father to the
Casino, it made me nervous
To watch him risking fairly
Large sums at chemin de fer
(He didn't like roulette)
But Geneviève went with him
In the evenings, when I
Was laboriously working
My way through Proust's
Ombre des jeunes filles
En fleurs in French. My
Father golfed in the
Afternoons, but I preferred
The beach, swimming and
Sitting with Geneviève
Under her pink beach umbrella.
She never went in the water.
We talked about everything
But mostly I drew on her
Knowledge of French literature.
It was she who first put me
Onto the incomparable love
Sonnets of Louise Labé and
The contemporary poetry of
Paul Eluard and Max Jacob.
In the Hispano-Suiza, with
Plumb still at the wheel, we
Made excursions to visit

The cathedrals of Reims and
Amiens, glorious structures
With fine medieval sculpture
Which had not been damaged
In the war. When it came
Time to return to the States
There was a lachrymose
Parting with Geneviève.
Young as I was, I had
Fallen in love with her.

In the following years there
Was no noticeable improvement
In my father's mental health,
Though sometimes there were
Brief interludes of normalcy
Between the downswing and the
Upswing. In one of these
I persuaded him to go to
Pittsburgh, reminding him
That he had a wife there and
Another son. He went and
Stayed for about a month
With them at the Woodland
Road house but it didn't
Work out. They got on each
Other's nerves and there
Was no renewal of the love
That had first drawn them
Together. It annoyed my
Father that my mother made
Him go to church and that,
At home, she kept badgering
Him to kneel down to pray

With her for his recovery.
My brother was ashamed of
Father's illness; he was
Hostile in various small
But annoying ways.

So, when he was entering
The manic phase, my father
Took off again for Florida.
When he had me down to visit
Him we had another great
Trip in the *Sarsho*,
Going all the way down to
Key West. I should add
That in a later year he
Had the boat trucked to
New Orleans. We went for
Several days through the
Spooky bayous, then
Turned around and went
North on the Mississippi
As far as Natchez to see
The splendid antebellum
Mansions of the planters.
When he was low he took
Refuge with his sister.
When he was high it was
Back to Europe, golfing
In Scotland and a long
Visit with Geneviève.
Then fate struck a cruel
And mortal blow. Walking
Across the busy Place
De la Concorde in Paris

Geneviève was hit by a
Car that was out of
Control and killed. My
Father was never able to
Forget her or bring himself
To return to France.

EZRA (POUND)

To Rapallo then I came,
That was in 1934, a student
Bored with the academic conventions
Of Harvard, wanting to get to the source,
To learn about poetry from the best
Poet alive, and you accepted me into
Your Ezuversity where there was no
Tuition, the best beanery since
Bologna (1088). Literachoor, you said,
Is news that stays news,
And quoting from some old bloke
Named Rodolphus Agricola,
Ut doceat, ut moveat, ut delectet,
Make it teach, move the heart,
And please. You taught me
And you moved me and you gave me
Great delight. Your conversation
Was the best show in town,
Whatever you'd ever heard or read
As fresh as when it first got into
Your head. The books you loaned me
Were full of caustic marginalia:

Fat-faced Frankie (meaning Petrarch)
Had an assistant to put the adjectives
In the lines, it didn't much matter
Where they were placed; and
Aristotle was Harry Stottle,
A logic-chopper but so good at his
Job he anchored human thought
For 2,000 years; and Aristophanes was
Harry-Stop-Her-Knees, good stuff about
Wasps and frogs. You believed
You were a revenant of Sextus
Propertius, your favorite Latin
Poet, saying that Propertius had
Rip-van-Winkled from 16 B.C. and you
Rewrote the best parts of your idol
In English, bringing the old boy's
Ideas up to date according to
Your own predilections. In your
Study, to keep from losing them,
You hung your glasses, your pens
And your scissors from strings
Over your desk. You had two
Typewriters because one was
Always being repaired from the
Beating you gave them; your
Letters were often half full of
Capitals for emphasis. You read
My poems and crossed out half the
Words saying I didn't need them.
You advised me not to bother
Writing stories because Flaubert
And Stendhal and James Joyce
Had done all that could be done
With fiction. They say you were

Cranky, maybe so, but only with
People who deserved it, stupid
Professors busy killing poetry
And international bankers making
Usury and *i mercanti di cannoni*
Selling arms to start another war.

You elucidated the Eleusinian
Mysteries which were a key part of
Your composite religion, all about
Dromena and the *epopteia* and how
It was the *epopteia* that sent sperm
Up into a man's brain to make him
Smart. You loved cats and the cats
Loved you. Some days we would
Walk up the stony *salite* on the
Mountainside behind town, through the
Olive groves and the little peasant
Farms where the cats were perched
On the stone walls; they were
Waiting for you, they knew you
Would bring them a packet of scraps
From the lunch table. You would
Call to the cats: *Micci, micci,*
Vieni qua, c' é da mangiare
("Here's something for you to eat").
One day when we were feeding the
Cats near the church of San
Pantaleone we discussed what you
Would do with your Nobel Prize
Money when you finally got it,
And you thought that a chef
Would be the best thing because
You were tired of eating at the

Albuggero Rapallo, but the Swedes
Never got around to giving it
To you, they were too dumb to
Understand the *Cantos*. And when
Henghes the sculptor (id est
Heinz Winterfeld Klusmann)
Walked all the way down from
Hamburg to Rapallo to see you
Because he heard you had known
Gaudier, and arrived half starved,
You fed him and let him sleep in
The big dog kennel on the terrace
(Since there were no extra beds in
The penthouse apartment) and
You took him to the yard of
The man who made gravestones
And got him credit for a block of
Marble, from which he carved
His sitting-down centaur, and you
Sold it for him to Signora Agnelli,
The Fiat lady in Torino; and that
Was the beginning of Henghes' fame
And good fortune (and the drawing for
The Centaur became the colophon for
New Directions). You said I was
Such a terrible poet, I'd better
Do something useful and become
A publisher, a profession which
You inferred required no talent
And only limited intelligence.

And after lunch you would
Stretch out on your bed with your
Cowboy hat shielding the light from

The window with the big Chinese
Dictionary on a pillow on your
Stomach, staring at the characters,
Searching for the glyph of meaning
In the calligraphy. And years
Later the professor asked your
Daughter to define your ideogrammic
Method of composition in the *Cantos*,
And she thought for a moment and
Replied that you looked deep into
The characters to find the truth of
Them, which was a properly Confucian
Answer. So you wrote your own
Versions of the *Great Learning*
And the *Odes*, which horrified
The Sinologists, but the language
Is immortal. And you loved to
Quote from Confucius that:
"Anyone can run to excesses, it is
Easy to shoot past the mark, it is
Hard to stand fast in the middle."

DAPHNE

The great love of my junior year
At Harvard was Daphne. Like her
Namesake, the nymph Daphne who
Was pursued through the forest
By the god Apollo, she was a
Delicate beauty. I saw her
First at one of the dances in

The Ritz. She was across the
Ballroom from me, sitting
Placidly beside the elderly
Lady who was her chaperone.
As I moved closer to her I
Noticed those enormous blue
Eyes which were to entrance
Me for many months. When I
Bowed and asked her to dance,
She demurred, saying that she
Wasn't a good dancer. "Go on
With you," the chaperone
Said, "you dance better than
I ever did." I took her hand,
Which was very cold. She was
So shy she wouldn't look at me.
Shyness as I found later was
Characteristic. Shyness and
Diffidence. What made her that
Way? She was very beautiful
And she was from one of the
Oldest Boston families, many
Generations of good breeding.
She didn't speak as we danced
And hardly smiled when I spoke
To her. But she danced well,
Light on her feet. It took
Me only a few minutes to realize
That someone important had come
Into my life.

My romance with Daphne was so
Totally different from anything
I had had before, when girls

Were little better than objects
To capture. For me she was
Indeed someone to be worshiped,
The nymph Daphne or even perhaps
A goddess. She was reluctant to
Give her telephone number but
The chaperone produced it.
The rather regal old lady had
Perhaps seen something in me.
I called for Daphne a few days
Later in one of the old houses
On Chestnut Street. A small
Bronze plaque on the door
Gave the name Sargent. An
Antiquated maid let me in
And put me in a hall chair.
"Miss Daphne will be down
Soon." It was Thursday so
We took a taxi to Symphony
Hall for the afternoon concert,
I felt proud to be escorting
Such a beautiful girl. Some
Dvořák was on the program
That Koussevitzky was
Conducting, one of my
Favorite composers. I told
Her they were playing him
In her honor. She turned
Those huge eyes toward me,
Telling me not to be silly.
Half an hour into the
Concert I tried to take
Her hand but she sternly
Pulled hers back. It was

Like a gesture of fear.
What had she to be afraid
Of? And so it was for
Several months: there
Could be no touching and
Certainly no kissing. She
Would go out with me but
On a very formal basis,
Almost the way it must
Have been in the last
Century. It happens that
My cousin Duncan Phillips
Wrote a book on the Renaissance
In which he featured Titian's
Sacred and Profane Love. Being
With Daphne the great painting
Came back to me with force.
Young as I was, had I given
Too much time to "profanity,"
Too much time pursuing
Easy, profane girls and
Not enough to the sacred
Ones? It was a crossroads.
I soon realized that I was
Seriously in love with Daphne,
The real thing, no doubt of it.

At first she didn't want to
Go out on evening dates. We
Went to the concerts and the
Museums, but she did like the
Theater though the fare was
Never good in Boston. Very
Often we went walking, on the
Common then along the Charles.

Having my car we could go out
To Concord to visit my cousins
Becky and Henry in their lovely
Place on the river. Daphne
Declined riding and swimming
But she enjoyed badminton and
Croquet. Becky was very good
At drawing her out of her
Shyness. "Your girl seems a
Bit confused, but she's a
Rare one," Becky told me.
Quite often we went out to
The Pickmans in Bedford. That
Was an intellectual household.
Dudley Pickman was a private
Scholar, devoting his life to
A history of Christendom in
The Fourth Century; whether
He ever finished it I don't
Know. He had a nice wit.
Hester Pickman was a Chanler
From the Genesee Valley up
Near Buffalo. A voracious but
Discriminating reader. She was a
Bluestocking right enough but a
Very amiable one. What drew
Daphne to the Pickmans was the
Two daughters of about her own
Age. They had all been to the
Fashionable Winsor School
Together. Daphne was at ease
With them, no shyness. She
Could laugh with them and play
With their dogs, an entirely
Different person.

I wrote often to my mother in
Pittsburgh and references to
Daphne became more frequent and
Enthusiastic. Finally I came out
With it that I'd like to marry
Daphne if she would have me
And if when I'd finished at
Harvard there might be an
Apartment for us on the third
Floor of 104 Woodland Road
And some sort of a job for me
In Pittsburgh. Needless to say
I'd said nothing about this
To Daphne yet. My mother took
The next train to Boston. Her
Visit to the house on Chestnut
Street was both disagreeable and
Comic. My mother always had
Pleasant manners with strangers
But Mr. Sargent was determined
Not to like her. His questions
About life in Pittsburgh were
Insulting, as if my native city
Were located somewhere out
In the Indian-infested plains
Beyond the Mississippi, with
An appropriate culture. Daphne
Was shaking with shame at her
Father's behavior. The tea
Party was rescued by the tact
And charm of Daphne's step-
Mother, an upper-class English
Woman named Phoebe. She had
Come to the house some years
Before to be governess for

Daphne and then, when Daphne's
Mother unexpectedly died,
Had been elevated to be
Mr. Sargent's wife. When tea
Was brought in Phoebe took
Charge of the conversation
Which became a laughing account
Of her youth in Somersetshire,
Laced with many amusing anecdotes
Of rural ways. Thanks to her
The ice was melted and Daphne
Stopped shaking. I could see
That my mother had taken to
Phoebe so I invited her to
Have dinner with us, including
Daphne of course, at Lochobers
In Winter Place, the home of
The tastiest lobsters. Happily
Old Grump declared that he
Would join his friends at the
Somerset Club. At the restaurant,
Having the purpose of her trip
In mind, my mother brought the
Topic around to young men and
Pronounced very sweetly that
They should not think of
Marrying until they had done
With college. Phoebe concurred
In that as did Daphne. I think
That for her, with her shyness,
The idea of marriage was very
Frightening. Daphne and I kept
On going about together, but
Always on the basis of *noli*
Me tangere.

T. S. ELIOT

A big literary event on the
Harvard campus that year was
T.S. Eliot's residency to give
The Norton Lectures, the
Highest academic honor that
The university bestows. The
Great man, of course, was
Given a suite in Eliot House
Where in the library his
Wyndham Lewis portrait frowns
Down on the readers. I had met
Eliot through Pound, if only
By correspondence, and was
Pleased to confirm that "Ole
Possum," as Pound called him
(Eliot called Pound "Br'er Rabbit")
Was very amiable for a High
Anglican. He allowed me to take
Him to lunch at the Signet
Which greatly elevated my
Standing in the club. Eliot
Had a ready sense of humor.
His group conferences with
Students took place in the
Large living room of his suite
With the lads in chairs around
The wall. I noticed that there
Was always a plate of cookies
On the floor in the middle of
The room. "It's economical," he
Told me, "they're too polite
To go out and grab cookies.

That plate has been there for
Five weeks." When Bill Williams
Came up to Cambridge I feared
A confrontation. Bill hated
Eliot's work, particularly
The Waste Land, which he had
Called traitorous because it
Sounded so English, Eliot
Having been born in St. Louis.
But Eliot was the perfect
Gentleman. He shook hands
Politely, said not a word,
And absented himself.

PORNOGRAPHY AT HARVARD

One morning in the spring
The Boston tabloid paper
Carried a disturbing head-
Line: PORNOGRAPHY AT
HARVARD. My friend John
Slocum and I were the
Culprits. John was the
President of the *Advocate*
That year and I was "Pegasus"
At his right hand. Some time
Before we had talked about
What could be done to liven
Up the magazine to increase
Circulation. We hit on the
Idea of inviting contributions
From outside the college

Community. We got a poem
From Archie MacLeish and a
New *Canto* from Pound. Then
Came the bombshell, a very
Funny piece from Henry
Miller. It was innocuous
But it caught the eye of a
Young lawyer who was running
For district attorney in
Cambridge. He passed it
Along to the press, stirring
Up a lot of publicity. The
Harvard dean couldn't have
Cared less but there was
Quite a brouhaha in Boston
And Cambridge. The sheriff of
Middlesex County raided the
Newsstands to confiscate
Copies of the magazine. The
Piece was entitled "Glittering
Pie." It was good, if mild
Miller. I'll quote from it
To show what we were involved
With in this ridiculous
Situation. In the end, the fuss
Blew over when we gave the
Troublesome lawyer two
Seats on the first-base line
For the Yale game.

At the burlesk Sunday afternoon I heard Gypsy Rose Lee
sing "Give Me a Lei." She had a Hawaiian lei in her hand and
she was telling how it felt to get a good lei, how even her
mother would be grateful for a lei once in a while. She said
she'd take a lei on the piano, or on the floor. An old-fashioned

lei, too, if needs be. The funny part of it was the house was almost empty. After the first half-hour everyone gets up nonchalantly and moves down front to the good seats. The strippers talk to their customers as they do their stunt. The *coup de grâce* comes when, after having divested themselves of every stitch of clothing, there is left only a spangled girdle with a fig leaf dangling in front—sometimes a little monkey beard which is quite ravishing. As they draw towards the wings they stick their bottoms out and slip the girdle off. Sometimes they darken the stage and give a belly dance in radium paint. It's good to see the belly button glowing like a glowworm, or like a bright half-dollar. It's better still to see them [eleven words deleted by the cautious *Advocate* editors]. Then there is the loudspeaker into which some idiotic jake roars: "Give the little ladies a hand please." Or else—"Now ladies and gentlemen, we are going to present to you that most charming personality fresh from Hollywood—Miss Chlorine Duval of the Casino de Paris." Said Chlorine Duval is generally streamlined, with the face of an angel and a thin squeaky voice that barely carries across the footlights. When she opens her trap you see that she is a halfwit; when she dances you see that she is a nymphomaniac; when you go to bed with her you see that she is syphilitic.

SKIING

One of the reasons that I
Went to Harvard instead
Of Princeton was for the
Skiing. It was a long drive,
Five to six hours, to get to
Our favorite mountains but

We often did it. We would
Load up my car with a friend
And some fair ones and take
Off, in New Hampshire to
Cannon Mountain or the trail
That leads up Mount Washington
Or more likely to Stowe in
Northern Vermont. Stowe
Had a chairlift that ran
Up a sizable mountain, where
We could have a lot of
Downhill running without
A hard climb to get it.
Stowe was very cold toward
The top but in those early
Days we could wear our
Coats (mine was a venerable
Raccoon coat of my father's)
On the up trip on the
Chair; the attendant would
Put it on a down chair and
We would find it waiting
For us when we reached the
Bottom. One day I had a
Mishap at Stowe. Some of
Us were racing down the
Steep seven turns. I got
Going too fast and became
Out of control. I was
Headed for the woods. I
Put out my hand to save my
Head and crashed, ending
Up with a broken hand that
Had to be taken to the
Hospital. No more skiing

For over a month. In those
Days the bindings were
Very primitive. A toe-iron
And a strap to the heel and
A spring up to the back
Of the boot. Nothing like the
Modern boots in which you
Feel you are encased in
Concrete. In Stowe our
Favorite place to stay
Was the Stroms'. Erling
Strom, who had been on
Norway's Olympic team in
His day, was a character,
Full of wonderfully witty
Anecdotes. And there was
A beautiful (but strictly
Chaste) daughter named
Siri. In late spring we
Would climb up, sealskins
Attached to the bottoms of
Our skis, to the Mount
Washington headwall, an
Awesomely steep slope
Which I never attempted.
But it was nice to sunbathe
Below the headwall watching
The foolhardy tumble down it.

◆

After my junior year the longing
For Europe, the life there and
All the cultures of the various
Countries I knew, so gripped me that

I asked for leave of absence to study
Abroad on my own. The dean
Raised no objection. The grades
On my card were not brilliant
But they were all above passing.
"Just let me know ahead when
You want to return," he said,
"So that we can find a place
For you."

RAPALLO AGAIN

I went back first to see Pound
And found his talk as
Fascinating as ever, though
His disagreeable prejudices,
The anti-Semitism and the
Faith in Mussolini's way of
Running Italy, had increased
Since I had last seen him.
I simply changed the subject
If he brought these topics
Up. I learned more about the
Greek and Latin classics from
Pound, and about the poetry
Of various other languages,
Including the Provençal, than
I could have learned in any
Single class at Harvard.
Pound had devoted half a
Lifetime to finding out
How poetry worked.

After three years away from
Rapallo I found one rather
Startling change. Almost all
Of the townspeople seemed to
Know about Ezra's liaison with
Olga Rudge and that he spent
Tuesday and Friday nights
At her apartment up the
Mountainside in San Ambrogio.

His wife Dorothy, whose
English income paid the
Bills, appeared to be taking
The situation with resignation.
Perhaps she was used to Ezra's
Wanderings. There is a poem
In Pound's *Personae* called
"Stele" which begins:
"After years of continence
He hurled himself into a sea
Of six women." Autobiographical?
Who knows. Poets don't always
Tell the truth. Dorothy was
A fragile beauty but she
Came of solid stock. The
Family house was in the
Posh Kensington district
Of London. Her father was
An able barrister who left
A tidy estate to Dorothy,
His only child. Her mother,
Olivia Shakespear, wrote
Half a dozen novels that
Were well received, her

Favorite subject being
Marriages that didn't work
Out. Her beauty attracted
The poet Yeats, who for a
Time made her his secret
London mistress.

Olga Rudge was as outgoing
As Dorothy was silent. She
Was born in Columbus, Ohio,
But her accent was English
Because her mother decamped
From Ohio when Olga was
A baby, supporting herself
Giving singing lessons. The
Musical strain was strong
in Olga. When grown up she
Became a violinist of
International standing.
It was at a recital in
Paris in 1924 that Pound
First saw her. He fell for
Her at once. She was
Ten years younger than
Ezra and very pretty. On my
First visit to Rapallo I
Had spotted her alone at
A café and picked her up. But
I was soon tipped off by one
Of Ezra's friends to leave
Her alone, she belonged to
Pound. Some thirty years
Later, when Dorothy and
Ezra were estranged and he

Made his home in Olga's
Little house in Venice,
We became good friends. She
Was a gallant spirit
Looking after the poet
In his illnesses.

Those were joyous days in
Rapallo. The rainy season
Was over and the Tigullian
Gulf was bathed in sunlight.
Pound was in top form.
The stream of his talk
On every conceivable topic
Was still unabated. The
Ezuversity was running
Full steam. I took
My meals with the
Pounds at the usual
"Albuggero Rapallo,"
As they called it, but
Of course I paid for
My fare. The monolithic
Stone head of Pound by
Gaudier still stood in the
Corner of the dining room.
(I believe it is now with a
Collector in Kansas, but
He has promised to bequeath
It to the National Gallery
In Washington.) After lunch
Ezra liked to take a walk
Up one of the stony *salite*
That lead up the steep little

Mountains back of Rapallo. He
Would bring scraps from
Lunch to feed to the cats
Which were waiting for him
On the stone walls of the
Olive orchards.

Then came the best part of
The day: swimming. We would
Rent a *pattino* (two small
Pontoons with two seats over
Them, one with oarlocks)
And row out beyond the
Sewage of Rapallo to clean
Water. Ezra was a strong
Swimmer. He would dive in
And come up like Proteus,
The water glistening on
His red beard. The further
Out Ezra rowed the more
Impressive the view became,
The rock cliffs of Zoagli
On the right to the peninsula
Of Portofino with its lighthouse
On the left. After our swim
Dorothy would give us tea in
Her large room in the penthouse,
A beautiful room, which brings
Back happy memories, for two
Reasons. The walls were lined
With the watercolors that she
Had done when she was a member
Of the Vorticist group;
Constructionist figures and

Abstract landscapes. And after
Ezra had gone to his typewriter
She would read aloud to me from
The stories of Henry James. Her
Kensington accent was just right
For James. I could imagine that
He was with us in Dorothy's
Room.

Before I left Rapallo Pound
Gave me a list of suggested
Places to visit on my travels.
As to be expected from him, it
Was a rather unconventional list,
Skipping Milan and Florence
And Rome. "Too many tourists,"
He said, and featuring some
Towns that he had written
About in the *Cantos*.

It would have been lonely going
Around by myself but by a
Miracle sexy, bubbly Lola had
Turned up. She had been my toasty girl
On my previous stay in
Rapallo, but I'd never
Had a letter from her after I
Went home. Lola, who liked
Now to be called Aurora, had
Been a torrid romance. She was
The daughter of the bank
Janitor, about fifteen or
Sixteen when I first met her,
But grown up beyond her years

In the intricacies of sex. We
Used to meet in a hidden
Undersea cave near the bathing
Cove. The most perfect body I
Have seen before or since. She
Could have served as model
For Apelles, the greatest of
The classic Greek painters.
From the night she picked me
Up she had been in love with
The idea of getting away
From Italy and I with her
Glorious body. Her story
Is told in my poem "In
Another Country." Inevitably
It had a sad ending for her.
But here she was again, news
Travels fast in Liguria,
And she bore me no malice
For having abandoned her
Before. *Noctes incredibiles.*
There were some mornings
On our trip when I was almost
Too worn out to drive.

Perugia, Siena, San Gimignano
In Tuscany. Gubbio, Arezzo,
Parma, Mantova, Brescia,
Assisi, Urbino, and Rimini,
Viterbo, Spoleto, and Ferrara.
A hodgepodge of an itinerary,
But I had rented a *topolino*
And there were little inns
Where we could spend the

Nights. The *autostrade* now
Connected the principal
Towns with tunnels through the
Mountains, a boon for the
Tourists but for me it meant
That old Italy was becoming
Motorized.

On our trip it was fun to
Have a pretty girl to instruct.
Lola was eager to learn some
English and I was amazed
At how much of the colloquial
She picked up in a few weeks.
I adjured her to correct my
Italian and she did, though
What she spoke was the dialect
Of Genoa and the Ligurian
Coast. She had a sense of
Humor. She had me memorize
What, in Genoa, you should
Say to recalcitrant cabbies.
It's still in my head:

> *Le prego di inghiottire*
> *un ombrello chiuso e di*
> *cacarlo aperto.*
> I pray you to swallow
> a closed umbrella and to
> shit it out open.

We saw interesting and
Wonderful things on Ezra's
List, but each of us had
His favorite. Lola liked

Mantova best, the towers
Of the town rising ghostly
Out of the surrounding lakes,
Then the huge palace of the
Gonzagas, 800 rooms of it,
With at the far end the
Little room with Mantegna's
Breathtaking frescoes.

My own favorites were
Urbino and the Tempio
Malatestiano at Rimini.
The upper part of Urbino,
Where the ducal buildings
Are, is quiet and peaceful;
Traffic is held to the busy
Lower part of the town.
Federigo da Montefeltro
(Whom Ezra called "half-nosed
Feddy" because in his portrait
By Piero della Francesca he
Is shown missing one eye
And with a great gouge at
The top of his nose). In
The fifteenth-century wars
Among the principalities he
Was one of the most renowned
Condottieri, a soldier of
Fortune fighting first for
One of the princes and then
For another. Yet he was a man
Of cultivation. He supplied
Patronage at his court for
A number of scholars, among

Them Baldassare Castiglione
Whose *The Book of the Courtier*
Is read in colleges to this
Day. Nor was he indifferent
To the visual. He had his
Portrait painted by good
Artists some dozen times,
And the intarsias (mosaics
Of varicolored strips of
Wood for wall decorations)
In the study of Feddy's
Palace are the finest in
Italy. One curious fact
About Feddy is that he
Hated books, didn't want
Them around. He maintained
A staff of thirty copyists
And calligraphers to provide
Him with his reading
Matter. I also liked
Urbino for a personal
Reason which was a sop
To my vanity. I was
Bargaining in a bookstore
For a book about Feddy
When the proprietor said:
"*Lei se difende bene in
Italiano.*" As my coach,
Lola was delighted with
That. He meant: "You defend
Yourself well in Italian."

One of the most famous, and
Also infamous, *condottieri*

Of the fifteenth century in
Italy was Sigismundo Pandolfo
Malatesta (1417–68), lord of
Rimini, Fana, and Cesena. He
Was brutal and treacherous,
But a remarkable soldier. At
The age of thirteen he led
The troops of Rimini in
Repelling a strong invader.
In maturity he was the ally
Of Francesco Sforza, the
Duke of Milan, in the wars
With Pope Eugenius IV. He
Married a daughter of the
Marquis of Ferrara, but
Three years after the wedding
He was accused of having
Her poisoned. Could it
Have been because he had
Fallen in love with Isotta
Degli Atti, the strong-
Willed woman who would
Dominate the rest of his
Life? Isotta had brains
And she knew how to
Handle a man.

But we did not come to
Rimini to track down
Isotta. We wanted to
Visit the extraordinary
Self-memorializing temple
Which the two of them had
Erected to their own

Glorification while still
Alive, the Tempio Malatestiano.
This magical building is
More of an architectural
Garden than a soul-lifting
Chartres or an overwhelming
St. Peter's. As a lover of
The classics, Sigismundo
Wanted a classical edifice
Where the "Goddess Isotta"
Could be enshrined as a
Grecian deity. He wanted
A pagan pantheon. And he
Found the man who could do
It for him in Leone Battista
Alberti, an architect who
Was enamored of the ancient
Architecture of Rome.

The origin of the Tempio
Was in the twelfth-century
Chiesa di San Francesco,
Built in Gothic style by
The Franciscans. At first
Sigismundo asked Alberti
To design two sepulchral
Chapels in the interior.
But as his fortune increased
He called for a new classical
Façade and complete design
Of the interior body of the
Church and decor to go with
It. The old church is not
Now visible in the nave.

The exterior is classical.
Within the main body of
The Tempio, along the walls,
Are separate chapels, each
One dedicated, with appropriate
Sculptural and pictorial
Decorations, to a separate
Significant personage.
Isotta's tomb is particularly
Fine. Two small elephants
Support the simulated marble
Coffin and above it are a
Baldachin and heraldic head.
Vertical small sculptures
Adorn the walls of the
Chapel. Throughout the
Tempio are many sculpted
Monograms of "I" and "S"
Decoratively linked.

Sigismundo's patronage
Attracted to the work
Some of the most eminent
Italian artists. There
Was Alberti, the architect,
And Matteo di Pasti, who
Supervised the building.
The finest of the sculptures
And bas-reliefs were done
By the Florentines Agostino
Di Duccio and Agnolo della
Stufa. In the reliquary
There is a large mural of
Sigismundo kneeling before

His ancestor St. Sigismundo,
King of Burgundy. In Isotta's
Chapel there is a magnificent
Large painted crucifix by
Giotto. Between the chapels
There are exquisite large
Bas-reliefs of mythological
Subjects: Diana the huntress,
The moon in her chariot, the
Queen of the angels, most of
These by Duccio. The motto
Of the Malatestas, frequently
Displayed on marble ribbons,
Is *Tempus Loquendi Tempus
Tacendi* (from Ecclesiastes;
"There is a time for speaking
And a time for keeping silent."
This doesn't seem to fit with
The violent Sigismundo, but
Like Federigo at Urbino, he
Had his humanist side and
Imported scholars to his court.
The most famous of them was
Gemisthus Plethon, a Byzantine,
Who inspired the teaching of
Plato in the Renaissance.
After Rimini we made a
Detour to see the miraculously
Preserved mosaics in the old
Church of San Vitale.

Lola had never seen art of
Such quality but she caught
On quickly and was agape

113

With admiration. It was very
Hard for me to put her on
The train to go back to
Rapallo. Quite apart from
Her fabulous concupiscence—
There was something new
Every night—she was good
Company. No arguments, just
Sweet companionship and
Lots of laughs about funny
Things that happened. I
Bought her some pretty
Dresses in a boutique in
Rimini. She gave me a lock
Of her hair. I promised her
I would be back in Rapallo
Before too long. But I'm
Afraid that was a lover's
Unkept pledge. It was years
Before I saw her again,
This time in Rome after she had
Married a nice man, a
Journalist for the *Eco di
Roma*. She was living with
Him in a spacious apartment
In the Via Caterina di Siena.
She wrote me when he suddenly
Died and I helped her out.
There has been a check for
Her every Christmas. "*Noi
Siamo stati regazzi felici
Quand' eramo insieme a
Rapallo, non e vero
Giacomino?*" "We were

Happy kids weren't we
When we were together
In Rapallo?" She had
Always called me Giacomino,
"Little James."

AUSTRIA

I gave up the *topolino* in
Italy and took the train
Through the Brenner to
Salzburg in Austria, one
Of my favorite places.
With the medieval castle
On its high perch of rock
Looming over the city,
And the sound of the
Salzach with its rapids
Murmuring day and night,
And the mountains of the
Salzkammergut in the
Background, it's a very
Poetic site. Happily,
The old part of Salzburg
Has not been modernized,
Though there is a McDonald's
Built to look like an old
House. *Salz* means "salt,"
And the history of the
Town goes back to the
Time when in the first

Century A.D. the Romans
Developed the neighboring
Salt mines. Its history
During the Renaissance
Was one of typical turmoil
As rival powers wrestled
For control. A more
Peaceful event was the
Birth of Mozart in 1756.
His *Geburtshaus* is the
Principal attraction for
Tourists. But a more musical
Tradition is carried on in
The summer operas of his
Work in the Festspielhaus
And the concerts of the
Mozarteum.

I had come to Salzburg to
Meet up with two friends,
Sandor Kerenyi and Koos
Vanderleou. Sandor was
Then a "stateless person,"
Traveling on a Nansen
Passport, because his
Native land (Transylvania)
And most of the family's
Wealth had been swallowed
By the Communists. I had met
Him skiing in Switzerland.
At the moment he was
Recuperating from a
Traumatic event. The past
Winter the girl with whom
He lived, despairing that

116

Sandor would ever marry
Her, jumped from the
Balcony of their rented
Chalet and had been killed.
Sandor, with his good
Looks and very haughty
Bearing, was irresistible
To women—of all ages—
Witness the comical story
Of his trunk. When Sandor
Was once living in a rather
Cramped one-room apartment
He persuaded an American
Lady of past middle age to
Store his wardrobe trunk
For him. But when he asked
To take the trunk back she
Declined, saying that if he
Wanted the trunk he should
Come to live with her. He
Never got the trunk with
His clothes in it. But
About a year later he had
Better luck. Skiing at
Klosters he met a French
Girl, the heiress of a
French company in paint,
Who took a shine to him
And before long they were
Married and Sandor was
Driving a Ferrari and
Living in a ritzy apartment
On the Avenue Foch in Paris.
All went well and in due
Course he had four children.

I met Koos Vanderleou, the
Dutch philosopher, when I
Was at Choate. He had come
There to give a lecture, and
I, as head boy in school, was
Delegated to show him around.
What a delightful man. He
Treated me like an equal and
We got on famously. Koos
Was from a family that had
Large plantations in Sumatra,
Which was a Dutch colony.
When I called him from Salzburg
He sent a car to bring
Me up to the Kammersee
Where he was renting a
House. The Kammersee is
One of the large lakes
That dot the upland
Region known as the
Salzkammergut. The shores
Of the lake are verdant with
Farmland. At the far end is
The Hirzberg mountain and
Beyond that big mountains in
The distance. An idyllic
Spot. When we reached the
Little Kammer village I was
Surprised to see that the
Houses of the vacationers
Were not built at the edge
Of the water but on long
Wooden piers that stretched a
Hundred feet into the lake.

When Koos took me out to
His house I was, more or
Less, surprised to find that
It had two mistresses, one
A handsome English girl,
A writer named Eugenia, and
Also an Austrian girl, the
Gräfin von Radstat. I
Assumed that the Austrian
Was a guest, but no, when
It was bedtime all three
Bedded down together in
A large Biedermeier bed.
In the morning Eugenia
Cooked a good English
Breakfast and the Austrian
Washed up. Everything
Serene, a happy family. It
Was the beginning of several
Pleasant days.

Days of complete relaxation
And fun, the sun broiling
Down on the lake, we were
In bathing suits most of the
Time. We ate our meals on
The pier, even in the
Evening it was so warm.
A few meters down the line
Was the house of Graf Ledebor,
Who lived with an English
Girl, Vanessa, who was a
Niece of the famous actor
Beerbohm Tree. She was

A smashing girl who kept
Us rollicking with stories
Of London life. Ledebor
Could have been an ad for
Atlas, the muscle man. He
Had an open speedboat and
Took us for scary rides
Down the lake with the
Spray flying. As always,
Koos's talk was absorbing.
I was particularly interested
In what he had to say about
Freud. No one was ever better
Adjusted to life than Koos,
But he had decided it was
Part of his research to
Be analyzed in the Berggasse.
His report was not favorable.
He had concluded that Freud
Was something of a fraud,
And that many of the
Symbolic dreams recounted
In his writings were
Of his own composition.
One day, to be serious,
We drove over to St.
Wolfgang to visit the
Fifteenth-century church
With its superb altar
Paintings by Michael
Pacher.

Of all my friends I was
Sure that Koos Vanderleou
Was destined for a

Long and tranquil old age.
He was healthy physically
And mentally. He enjoyed
Life with his lovers and
Friends. But that was not
The will of the gods. For
Years he had loved flying
In a little one-engined
Plane—a Cessna I think
It was—and was a good
Pilot. But he liked to
Do adventurous things. All
Of a sudden, a few years
After my visit with him
On the Kammersee, the
Fantasy hit him that it
Would be a good stunt to
Fly solo from Rome to South
Africa. A storm came on over
The Atlas Mountains. The wreck
And his body were found by
Berbers. I mourn him to this
Day, a star among men.

I hated to leave Koos and his
Entourage at the Kammersee
But I'd made a date for some
Climbing on bigger mountains
With my old friend and ski
Guide Eberhart Kneisel with
Whom I'd skied in past years.
I took the Vienna train from
Salzburg traveling east down
The Inn valley, and getting
Off at the small town of

Ötz. Then came the long and
Boring hike up the Ötz
Valley to the hut at its
Summit where Eberhart would
Be waiting for me. I had
Checked my suitcase at the
Ötz station and packed a
Few essentials in a back-
Pack. Even that much weight
Seemed too much for my hike,
Ten kilometers to the hamlet
Of Untergurgl, then as much
To Obergurgl, where I renewed
Myself with a delicious
Kaiserschmarren (a sweet omelet)
Produced by an old woman in
One of the peasant houses
Of whose Tyrolean dialect
I couldn't understand a word.
When I finally made it
To the hut, which sits on
The flank of the peak to
Protect it from the wind,
There was Eberhart waiting
For me and, typically, sitting
On a rock playing his harmonica.
He is an Olympic-class ski
Racer and a renowned rock
Climber, but perhaps he
Is best known for the tunes
He can coax out of his
Little harmonica: folk
Songs, jazz, even classical
Music. He wanted to set

Right off on a climb but
I told him I was fagged
Out after my hike. The
Alpine mountain huts are
Well stocked with drink
As well as food, which is
Cooked for the visitors
By a hut mistress, so we
Had a few bottles of
Beer. I wish we had huts
Like these in the mountains
In America. They are a
Blessing. They mean that,
Summer or winter, on
Foot or on skis, you can
Tour in the high country
Without having to pack
Your food. The huts are
Supplied in summer by men
Of the villages below. And
The prices are very modest.
To be sure there are no
Soft beds. One sleeps
On the floor of the
Matratzenlager where
Straw pallets and often
Somewhat odoriferous army
Blankets are provided
(Pillows or sleeping bags
Are extra). There is a
Special feature of the
Öztal hut which is not
Listed in the guidebooks.
The hut overhangs an Italian

Village about a thousand
Feet lower, and often young
Women of dubious virtue
Will climb up to it to
Entertain the visitors
Of an evening.

In the ensuing days of
Good weather Eberhart
Led me on some very
Pleasant climbs. He was
The perfect guide for me
Because he never tried
To push me beyond my
Limits. I'm not good
On difficult rock and
Never will be. It's no
Fun for me to trap
Myself in a couloir
That has inadequate
Finger holds. Eberhart
Always roped me and that
Alleviated my fears. I'm
Not that famous English
Climber who wrote in his
Book—I forget his name
Now—that he "clung to
The face of the Eigerwand
By gripping a spillikin
Of rock in his teeth
When hands and toes were
Taken until he was rescued
By a rope from the rescue
Party up above." The

Eigerwand that looms over
Scheidegg in Switzerland
Has been the great killer
Of climbing. The last time
I was skiing in Scheidegg
I could look up to the
Sheer face and see three
Dead bodies swinging on
Their ropes in the wind,
Climbers who could not
Be rescued. None of that
Folly for Eberhart. Roped
To him it was sheer pleasure
And no fear. In the days
I was with him we did half
A dozen adjacent peaks.
The views out to the Silvretta
Range and the Tauerns were
Spectacular. We would sit
By the summit poles, and
Out would come the harmonica.
Evenings in the hut after
One of the hut mistress's
Good meals—how did she
Make them so tasty when
She had only frozen meat
And a little pot stove
To work with—we would
Play *Zwei Groschen* poker
With other guests, but
Go early to the pallets.

OLGA

When I first came to Rapallo
In the fall of 1934 to study
In Pound's "Ezuversity," I
Didn't know my way around or
Who was who. So when I spotted
A very good-looking young lady
Sitting by herself at a café
Table I didn't hesitate to
Ask if I might join her. She
Was vivacious and told good
Anecdotes about Max Beerbohm
And other famous personalities
Who had lived in Rapallo. I
Was puzzled by her accent
And asked if she were English.
No, she said, she had been
Born in Youngstown, Ohio,
But the family had moved to
England when she was quite
Young. I sat with her other
Days but noticed that she was
Never at her table on Tuesdays
Or Fridays. I learned more a
Few weeks later when I had
Become friendly with Gerhart
Münch, the young German
Pianist whom Pound had urged
To settle in Rapallo to play
In the concerts Ezra sponsored
In the *municipio*. "*Weisst du
Nicht, dass diese Dame das
Besitztum Ezrasist?*"..."Don't you

Know that the lady belongs
To Ezra?" A fact which was
Confirmed a few days later
When I happened to be in the
"Main drain" of the town,
The first big street back
The seafront plazas.
There came Ezra, dressed
To the nines in his velvet
Jacket, pants with equestrian
Seat, his cowboy hat, swinging
His silver-headed cane as he
Made for Sant' Ambrogio, women
Applauding him from their
Windows. It was one of the
Sights of the town. Olga,
That was her name, lived up
The mountainside, renting
The first floor of a peasant
House near the little church
Of San Pantaleone. The view
Up there over the Ligurian
Gulf was marvelous and the
Whole area was covered with
Olive trees. There were no
Car roads up there then; the
Climb up the stony *salita*
Was arduous. Ezra's concerts
In the town hall were very
Fine. Olga, with her violin,
Was the lead player, with
Münch and occasional imported
Talent filling in. The
Program was usually Mozart
And Vivaldi, Olga's favorite

Composer. Vivaldi was the
Master of Italian Baroque
Music. In later years she
Became a scholar of Vivaldi,
Researching his unpublished
Scores in Turin and Dresden.
She turned up over 300 unplayed
Vivaldi concerti, arranging to get
Some of them published.

That first year I was never
Invited up to the love nest
In Sant' Ambrogio, Ezra wanted to
Keep his life with Olga separate
From that with his wife Dorothy
Down in Rapallo, but in later
Years I got to know her well.
My most vivid memories were
Of a trip to look in on their
Daughter Mary who was farmed
Out with a rural family, the
Marchers, up near Bressanone in
The Italian Tyrol. Ezra was
Satisfied that the Marchers
Were good foster parents for
His child because Herr Marcher
Hung his pants on the crucifix.
Our big trip in a car I had
Rented was up into Austria.
Our first stop was in the
Town of Wörgel, where the
Deposed mayor, Herr Unter-
Guggenberger, had attempted
To institute *Schwundgeld*, one
Of Ezra's prescriptions for

Economic reform. This visit
Is recounted in *Canto 74*.
Then we drove on to Salzburg,
Where we put up at an inn
Called the Goldene Rose
Which had bedbugs. Salzburg
Was the scene of one of
Ezra's most eccentric
Pronouncements. Ezra had
Always hated the music of
Beethoven, but we lured him
To go to the Festspielhaus
To hear Toscanini conduct
Fidelio. After fifteen minutes
He rose up in his seat and
Called out: "What can you
Expect, the man had syphilis."
And we stalked out. Toscanini
Didn't miss a beat. Olga gave
Ezra complete support in his
Economic theories.

With the help of her father
Olga was able to buy a small
House in Venice near the
Salute. This became Ezra's
Home in his later years when
He had separated from Dorothy.
The care she gave him in the
Years when he had gone into
His silent period, speaking
To no one except her, was of
Exceptional devotion. She
Kept him going when his health
Was failing and he had given

Up writing. Sometimes, she
Told me, it took her till
Noon to get Ezra out of bed
And ready for his breakfast.
If there were guests he would
Sit taking in the conversation,
Rubbing his hands together as
A penance but never speaking.

Another place where I knew
Olga was in Siena, the
Very beautiful unspoiled
Medieval town in Tuscany.
Count Chigi Saracini, his
Was one of the oldest noble
Families in Italy, gave
Olga a nice position as
Assistant and hostess for
The summer musical festivals
Which he sponsored. She did
Her job well, keeping a flock
Of performers and singers from
Many countries happy. It was
Thanks to Olga that I had
The privilege of sleeping
For a night in a bedroom in
The Palazzo Chigi that had
An original Botticelli on
Its wall. Siena was a sacred
Place for Ezra because of an
Ancient bank, the Monte dei
Paschi which, way back, Duke
Leopold of Siena had founded,
With a charter providing

That not more than 3%
Interest be charged to the
Peasants, an exemplar
To Ezra that honesty could
Overcome usury. Siena was
The site of the annual race
Of the Palio when teams
Of citizens in costume
Raced their horses around
The central square.

Once there was a surprise
Visit in New York from Olga
And Ezra. The office phone rang
Saying, "Here we are, Jas," and
Indeed they were, staying at a
Little hotel in the Forties, which
She said had been very nice in her
Youth but now it was a place for
Prostitutes. I hastened to move
Them down to our apartment in the
Village. Ezra had been invited
To attend the annual meeting of
The Academy of American Poets,
And Olga had coaxed him to come
Over for it. At the ceremonial
Ezra was placed on a throne
In a big room at the Public
Library. He was a regal figure
But spoke to no one except his
Old friend Marianne Moore. A
Few days later I drove them
Up to one of his alma maters,
Hamilton College, where I

Was to receive a degree, largely
Because I was his publisher.
He got a big hand marching in
The academic parade but was
Totally silent. But he did
Utter a few words when we were
Driving to Norfolk, but they
Were the saddest I ever heard.
We stopped for dinner along
The road, but when it was
Time to go there was no Ezra.
He had wandered off into the
Woods. What he said was, "Why
Don't you discard me, Jas,
Then I won't be any more
Trouble to Olga." The
Saddest words. Olga was
Taking care of Ezra when
He died in Venice in 1972.
She lived on with her daughter
Mary at Brunnenburg until
1996.

For his final tribute
To Olga Ezra had prepared
These lines to go in the
Last of the *Cantos*:

That her acts
        Olga's acts
                of beauty
        be remembered.

Her name was courage
& is written Olga.

TONI OR NINI?

And to think I danced with your
Great-aunt the night of the
Anniversary ball in the Liechten-
Stein Palais, a pretty little
Thing she was, name of Toni
For Antonia and a bit saucy.
There was a powdered-wig, knee-
Britched footman standing still
As a ramrod on each step of the
Marble staircase from the entry
Hall up to the ballroom,
Motionless as a statue, never
Twitching an ear; manpower was
Cheap in those days. Or was
Her name Nini? There were two
Cousins who were almost look-
Alikes, both of them dark and
Beautiful waltzers. And old
Liechtenstein had to be in a
Wheelchair; he had potted
Himself in the foot shooting
Pheasants on his place in
Bohemia. Not a bad sort for
A man that rich, and all those
Old paintings worth a fortune
In the castle at Vaduz. Toni
Or Nini, which was it, Toni
Or Nini?

MY AUNT

Most mornings at Robin Hill
When I was living there on the
Third floor, that was before
My first marriage and when the
Office of New Directions was in
Her converted stable, she would
Summon me to her second-floor
Sitting room after breakfast and
Sit me down by the fireplace for the
Daily monologue which usually
Went on for at least an hour,
Without interruption for I wasn't
Expected to say anything, just to
Listen and absorb her wisdom about
Life, of which there was a large
Supply. This sounds very boring
But it wasn't; it was endlessly
Fascinating. How had nature or
Some divine agent packed into
This little woman (she was my
Father's sister) such an intensity
Of feeling and such a capaciousness
Of spirit. She would have been in
Her sixties then and there she sat
In her Chinese silk peignoir
At the little table by the window
That looked out over the gardens
(She had attended a horticultural
School; in those days young ladies

Were not sent to college). There,
She looked out at her beautiful gardens,
After she had finished her breakfast
Which consisted only of one uncooked
Egg which she downed in a gulp.
There I was, slumped in an easy
Chair (I was forbidden to smoke
In her presence) waiting for the
Lesson to begin, impatient to have
It over so I could get on with my
Writing but curious to know what
Would come from the lips of the
Oracle that day. And once she began
I was in thrall to her conviction.

These scholia took place long, long
Ago. My aunt has been dead for over
Thirty years. The great house and
Its gardens have passed out of the
Family. I am older than she was
When she was my teacher. Yet even
Now as I sit here typing, her figure
Is as clear as if she were still
Alive; she is standing in the doorway
Of my study, the not beautiful little
Woman with the insistent voice.
Her consuming love for me has
Penetrated time, it surrounds me
Like a sacred aura. She had great
Need of me, imperfect as I was.
She had no children of her own,
And I was named for the father
Whom she idolized. I was the
Receptacle. She was determined to put
As much of him into me as she could.

She had a store of stories to tell me
About her parents and the aunts and
Uncles, even about my great-grandfather,
Who looks so fierce in the daguerreotypes
In the family album; about his house
Where wide lawns sloped down to the
Allegheny River as it came through
Pittsburgh to join the Monongahela
To make the Ohio at the Point where
Once Fort Duquesne had stood. Trips
In the buggy with her father to the
New mills on the South Side, where the

Eliza Furnaces were named for one of
Her aunts, the flames rising out of
Them against the sky at night.

Character studies of beloved servants,
Irish if they were "inside," black if
They were "outside." When the riverfront
Property was sold to make way for
Joseph Horne's department store, a new
House, rather ugly, was built on
Lincoln Avenue in Allegheny, which
Was becoming a fashionable neighborhood
For the quality. And much she had to
Tell about her father's place near
Zellwood in the central lake country
Of Florida. It had begun as pine and
Palmetto land for shooting quail; then
He developed it into orange groves
And an elaborate estate. "Sydonie"
He called it, named for his wife
Sydney Page. There were avenues
Bordered with live oaks and flowering
Shrubs. There were trees brought from
Many parts of the world; greenhouses
And slat houses. A dairy herd of
Jersey cows. There was a power plant
And an aviary of exotic birds. Two
Small lakes and a boathouse. Twenty
Cabins (without plumbing) where the
Black workers lived. (Remember that
All this was built before there was
An income tax.) The house was in
Spanish style, white walls and
Red tile roofs copied from a villa

137

In Granada; terraces and courtyards,
Balconies and colonnades, bougainvilleas
Climbing the walls, separate apartments
For the families of each of the
Five children. There was, of course,
A track spur at the Zellwood station
For the parking of private cars.
(Today the place is a boarding school
For the children of missionaries.
Came the income tax and it couldn't
Be kept up.) The *Ariadne* was her
Father's two-masted schooner, crew
Of twelve, one of the prides of the
New York Yacht Club cruise. Each
Summer the cruise put in at
Nantucket harbor for a few days of
Onshore partying. That was where
My aunt met her consort, a Coffin
He was, a gentleman through and
Through, *sans peur et sans reproche.*
It was a long and happy marriage but
Without issue: the country gentleman
And the lady who loved gardens.

In her later years my aunt became
Interested in spiritualism. Through
A medium in Pleasantville she met
An angel in the beyond named Lester.
Lester was most sympathetic to the
Concerns of cultivated elderly
Ladies. It was a fervid correspondence.
My aunt would telephone her questions
To Pleasantville where they were
Communicated to Lester in séances,

His answers reached Robin Hill in
The medium's automatic writing. She
Consulted him about almost everything,
Except her investments which were in
The care of a banker in New York. The
Problems of all the young cousins
Whom she was educating, difficulties
With the servants, social problems,
Matters of conscience, her husband's
Health — it all went to Lester. It's
Clear from Lester's letters (I have
Them still) that he really cared,
Particularly for what they called
"Going on to greater understanding."
Reading over some of the letters
I find that Lester's advice was very

Good; he was a sensible angel. He
Was a great consolation to her. At
A certain point, when I was giving
Her a hard time, I became the subject
Of the exchange. She told him that
She was much worried about me. I was
Making girls fall in love with
Me with no intention of marrying
Them; what was to be done?
Lester's answer was very comforting
And rather accurate as I read it now
In the medium's jiggly script: "Don't
Worry, my dear, James will be all
Right; you have given him good
Values. It is normal for young men
To flirt, it's their nature. He will
Settle down soon and when the right
Girl comes along he will know it
And will make a good marriage. He
Will work hard and be a success in
His profession."

She went on to greater under-
Standing in her 86th year. The
End was hard for her but she bore
It stoically. There were more voices,
A clamor of Babel; a coming on of
Darkness, a struggle to hold the
Light; confusion and desperation;
Then bodily failures, waning of
Strength; days in silence, barely
Able to speak; the soul fighting
For life in her eyes; inanition.
Two of her men, young Leon and old

Theodore Sylvernale, the old man
Weeping, placing her gently on the
Wicker chaise longue; her black
Maids who grew up on the family
Place in Florida covering her
With blankets; she is carried, an
Egyptian mummy, out into the sun
In her garden to lie there for
An hour. She says nothing and
Seems to see nothing, moves not
Even her hand, is no longer a
Person.

REMEMBERING
WILLIAM CARLOS WILLIAMS

9 RIDGE ROAD

A not large, unpretentious
Wooden house, the clapboards
Painted a dull mustard color,
Two stories and an attic, set
On a little slope over the
Street level, with steps and
An iron railing going up;
By the door was a small sign:
9 Ridge Road. W.C. Williams,
MD. Please ring bell. The house
Must have been built at about
The time of World War One
And stands on an avenue of
Maple trees where the little
Business center of Rutherford
(NJ) merges into an area of
Comfortable homes inhabited
By commuters to New York,
Middle-class people mostly.
No superhighways in those
Days; by bus it was a boring
Hour's journey across the
Wetlands to Manhattan.

To this shrine, a supplicant,
I came a year after Pound had
Coaxed me into trying to become
A publisher, promising to write
His friends who might have books
That needed doing. William Carlos

Williams! What a magical name,
Was one to whom he had written.
I was a-tremble to barge in on
One of my literary idols, who
Was not yet famous with the general
Public, but in the underground
Of the literary avant-garde,
Such as we'd heard about in
Boarding school, along with
Pound, he was supreme. *Kora in
Hell* and *Spring and All* had
Been sacred texts in Dudley
Fitts's honors class at Choate.
I was afraid that Williams when
He saw how young I was would
Send me packing. What would he
Be like? I climbed the steps and
Rang the bell. A woman opened.
This would be Floss, his wife,
Telling me the doctor was with
A patient, to take a seat in the
Parlor, I was expected. A very
Ordinary room, somewhat shabby
Furniture. But the paintings
On the walls: a cubist Demuth
Of industrial smokestacks and
Two slender Demuth flowers; a
Precisionist Sheeler bowl of
Fruit; a Dove and a Marin; a
Colorful Ben Shahn abstraction
Of a building that seemed to be
All eyes. These were gifts from
His painter friends. Also a
Marsden Hartley, pale mountains

**KORA IN HELL
IMPROVISATIONS**

By WILLIAM CARLOS WILLIAMS

144

In New Mexico. Later on Bill
Told me that Hartley had been
A pest, trying to make passes.

After a wait the doctor came in
With his white coat on, a big
Smile, very welcoming. Without
Reserve he told me an anecdote
About the patient he had just
Been treating. All doors were
Open. Bill was a noncutaneous
Man. No skin separated him from
Others. A new acquaintance was
At once a friend. He had no
Side. His speech was broken now
And then by an extraordinary goat
Laugh. Floss joined us, a small
Sturdy woman, serious, laconic.
She did not smile too easily.
She suffered from a buzzing in
One ear, the result of a whip-
Lash when Bill was driving the
Car and had to put on the brakes
Suddenly. Patient, enduring Floss.
Being married to such a bundle
Of energy as Bill couldn't have
Been easy for her.

Bill and I first talked about
Pound, they had been friends
In college. What was the old
Nut up to now? Then about Bill's
Two sons, Paul and William
Eric, one still in school, one

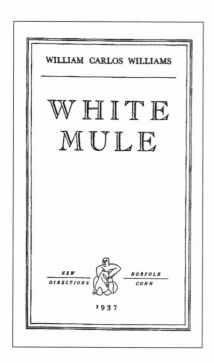

WILLIAM CARLOS WILLIAMS

WHITE MULE

NEW DIRECTIONS   NORFOLK CONN

1937

Starting college. Neither much
Interested in writing, and just
As well too, hardly a career
To recommend to a son, all
That grief he'd had getting his
Early books published. Twenty
Years ahead of what was then
Accepted by most readers. Bill
Had had to pay for publication
Of his first five books: the
Poems of 1909 (sold for 35¢
And not many sold at that, in
Garroway's Stationery store),
Al Que Quiere!, *Kora in Hell*,
Spring and All and *The Great
American Novel* (which wasn't
A novel at all). And when he
Finally found a commercial
Publisher to do his *Voyage to
Pagany*, the firm went bankrupt.
So Bill was desperate, he was
Willing to take a chance on
A 22-year-old neophyte. We
Decided that *White Mule*, his
Novel in which Floss is born on
The first page would be our
Beginning, and from there we'd
Go on to its sequels, the Stecher
Trilogy, which tells the history
Of Floss's German immigrant
Family. Before I left 9 Ridge
Road Floss and Bill took me to
See their flower garden, a small
Plot behind the kitchen stoop.

147

To Be

(Floss's birth, the opening lines of
White Mule)

"She entered, as Venus from the sea,
dripping. The air enclosed her, she felt
it all over her, touching, waking her. If
Venus did not cry aloud after release
from the pressures of that sea-womb,
feeling the new and lighter flood
springing in her chest, flinging out her
arms—this one did. Screwing up her
tiny smeared face, she let out three
convulsive yells—and lay still."

The Locust Tree in Flower

Among
the leaves
bright

green
of wrist-thick
tree

and old
stiff broken
branch

ferncool
swaying
loosely strung—

come May
again
white blossom

clusters
hide
to spill

their sweets
almost
unnoticed

down
and quickly
fall

This was Bill's favorite hobby.
Over a hundred poems on
Flowers and trees may be found
In his books. A florilegium.

On October 27, 1936, what a
Momentous day for me and for
New Directions, I found at
The post office a letter that
Was addressed to the deity.
"Dear God," it began, "You
Mention, casually, that you
Are willing to publish my
White Mule, that you will pay
For it and that we shall then
Share, if any, the profits!
My God! It must be that you
Are so tall that separate
Clouds circle round that head
Giving thoughts of other metal
Than those the under sides of
Which we are in the habit of
Seeing." *White Mule* was a
Success; Bill's first and my
First. Good critics reviewed
It. The book was talked about.
We did a second printing. I
Could walk into a shop with my
Wares and not be regarded as a
Crazy young freak. Bill's fame
Rubbed off on his old friend
Pound, whose books soon began
To move a bit as they had not
Before. A door opened. A new
Period in American literature

148

Began. We went to press with
Bill's stories, *Life Along the
Passaic River*, and not long after
With a *Collected Poems*.

On a later visit to 9 Ridge Road
Bill walked me up the hill back
Of his house. From the top there
Was a wide and open view across
The wetlands to the skyscrapers
Of Manhattan which rose like
White flowers through the haze.
In his early years New York City
Was a tantalizing enigma, "a
Dream of love and of desire,"
He called it in one poem, "a
Dream a little false." It was a
Menacing illusion. When he was
Interning at French Hospital
On 10th Avenue, then at Child's
Hospital uptown, Bill thought
About a lucrative practice in
The city. Manhattan was where
Writers and artists lived; he
Made many friends among them
In Greenwich Village. But he
Found other things he didn't
Care for. Ceaseless movement.
Corruption. Greed. Violence.
Tensions. The sense grew in him
That the area where he had grown
Up—Rutherford and the other
New Jersey towns around Paterson—
Was his *locus mirabilis*, where
He belonged and would be happiest,

From *Perpetuum Mobile: The City*

> —a dream
> we dreamed
>   each
> separately
>   we two
>
> of love
>   and of
> desire—
>
> that fused
> in the night—
>
> in the distance
>   over
> the meadows
>   by day
> impossible—
>   The city
> disappeared
>   when
> we arrived—
>
>   A dream
> a little false
>
> toward which
>   now
> we stand
>   and stare
> transfixed—
>
> All at once
>   in the east
> rising!
>
>   All white!
>   small
> as a flower—
>
> a locust cluster

...

a dream
        toward which
we love—
at night
      more
than a little
      false—

Complaint

They call me and I go.
It is a frozen road
past midnight, a dust
of snow caught
in the rigid wheeltracks.
The door opens.
I smile, enter and
shake off the cold.
Here is a great woman
on her side in the bed.
She is sick,
perhaps vomiting,
perhaps laboring
to give birth to
a tenth child. Joy! Joy!
Night is a room
darkened for lovers,
through the jalousies the sun
has sent one gold needle!
I pick the hair from her eyes
and watch her misery
with compassion.

The place where he was destined
To do his doctoring and also
Try to capture in his poetry
The sounds of the local speech
And the small-town folkways.
How did Bill manage to be a
Full-time pediatrician as well
As an obstetrician: hospital
Hours, office hours? House
Calls, night calls? And then
To write some thirty books on
Top of that. Drafting poems
On prescription slips as he
Drove in his car, writing
Stories on yellow pads as he
Waited for a woman to give
Birth, going up to his desk
In the attic to type for an
Hour or so after a night call.
Of course he had great strength
And vitality. But in the end
He paid for the drain on his
Body; he paid with the strokes
That crippled him in old age.
The secret was, I'm sure, that
His careers were complementary;
They fed on each other; together
They nourished him. He himself
Explains it thus in the chapter
"Of Medicine and Poetry" in his
Autobiography: "They ask me how
I have continued an equal interest
In medicine and the poem. I reply
That they amount for me to nearly

The same thing. The cured man
Is no different from any other.
It is a trivial business unless
You add the zest to the picture.
So it was that I came to
Find writing such a necessity.
My medicine was the thing that
Gained me entrance to secret
Gardens of the self. I was
Permitted by my medical badge
To follow the poor, defeated
Body into the gulfs and grottos.
Just there, the thing in all
Its greatest beauty may for
A moment be freed to fly
Guiltily about the room.
For a split second it has
Fluttered before me, a
Phrase which I quickly
Write down on anything at
Hand, any piece of paper
I can grab."

In 1912 Bill was married to
Florence Herman, the younger
Of two sisters. She had thought
He would marry her older sister,
Charlotte, but he was turned
Down. In frustration he courted
The younger girl. It is reported
That Bill told Floss that he
Didn't yet really love her but
In time he would. Hardly a very
Romantic proposal. "She must

From *Asphodel, That Greeny Flower*

"...
    At the altar
        so intent was I
before my vows,
    so moved by your presence
        a girl so pale
and ready to faint
    that I pitied
        and wanted to protect you.
As I think of it now,
    after a lifetime
        it is as if
a sweet-scented flower
    were poised
        and for me did open.

...an odor
    as from our wedding
        has revived for me
and begun again to penetrate
    into all crevices
        of my world."

From *Many Loves*

"Women! With their small
heads and big lustrous
eyes. All my life I have
never been able to escape
them."

Take him as he was, a poet, and
Together they'd work it out."
Which is what happened. Many
Years later when in old age
Bill wrote "Asphodel, That
Greeny Flower," the poem that
Was his final declaration of
Love for Floss and his apology
For his infidelities, he had a
Different view of their marriage.
It's common knowledge that
Bill had affairs; not to
The degree of womanizing,
Not satyriasis. He simply
Liked women, drew material
For his work from them. And
Women very much liked him.
After I'd first taken my wife,
Ann, to 9 Ridge Road she told
Me, "That is the most sexy
Man I think I've ever met."
He was kindly and enticing.
Perhaps it came from his mix
Of English and Spanish blood:
English father and Spanish
Mother from Puerto Rico. Bill
Didn't suppress his problem.
He felt guilty about it, he
Hated to hurt Floss, but
Bill's remorse, though it is

Clouded, comes through in his
Play *A Dream of Love*. It is
A double dream. In the first,
Dr. Thurber, physician and poet,
takes a neighbors's young wife
To a hotel in New York. Making
Love, he has a heart attack
And dies. In the second dream
He returns to the kitchen of
His home to explain what he
Has done to his grief-stricken
Wife. The explanation is in
Two parts. the first sets out
The role of woman in imagination,
The second, which must have been
Hard for Floss to take, suggests
That an occasional adultery is
Necessary to renew the fervor
Of connubial love.

I

Doc: "A man must protect his integrity as a man, as best he is able, by whatever invention he can cook up out of his brains or his belly. He must create a woman of some sort from his imagination to prove himself. It's a woman—even if it's a mathematical formula for relativity. Even more so in that case—but a woman. All right, a poem. I mean a woman, bringing her up to the light, building her up and not merely of stone or colors or silly words, but in the flesh, warm, agreeable, made of pure consents.

"And just as a woman must produce out of her female belly to complete herself—a son—so a man must produce a woman, in full beauty out of the shell of his imagination and possess her, to complete himself also . . . "

II

Myra: "I don't care what you do but I demand that you tell me what you promised this woman before you dropped dead in bed with her."

. . .

Doc: "Darling, don't let that bother you. I knew that if we were to keep on loving each other something had to be done about it. An opportunity offered itself and I took it. To keep love alive. . . . It went all right. I loved you as a consequence, more than I ever loved you in my life up to that time. It worked. I couldn't tell you—you couldn't have understood what I felt."

153

This Is Just to Say

I have eaten
the plums
that were
in the icebox

and which
you were probably
saving
for breakfast

Forgive me
they were delicious
so sweet
and so cold

And Floss's reply

Dear Bill: I've made a
couple of sandwiches for you.
In the icebox you'll find
blueberries—a cup of grapefruit
a glass of cold coffee.

On the stove is the teapot
with enough tea leaves
for you to make tea if you
prefer—Just light the gas—
boil the water and put in the tea

Plenty of bread in the breadbox
and butter and eggs—
I didn't know just what to
make for you. Several people
called up about office hours.

See you later. Love. Floss.

Please switch off the phone.

We get a clearer picture of
Domestic affection at 9 Ridge
Road if we look at what I
Call the "icebox poems." When
Floss or Bill wanted to leave
A message for the other a note
Would be pasted up on the door
Of the kitchen refrigerator.

And there was Cynthia, that
Vivacious girl, who worked
For Capezio's (they made shoes
For ballet dancers) and lived
In Charles Street in the Village,
Announcing with embarrassment
That she was knocked up and
Most likely it was mine. Hardly
A case for my family doctor.
Bill thought it was funny. He
Found an old Italian woman in
Hohokus who took care of the
Matter for $200. Luckily she
Knew her stuff, there were no
Complications. Cynthia settled
Down and married a nice young
Professor at CCNY.

For a man of such manic energy
Bill was even-tempered. He was
Not quarrelsome; he wore a
Mantle of lovable good humor.
In his arguments with his old
Friend Ezra Pound, who was
Forever badgering him about
Something, he was patient and

154

Indulgent. But there was one
Surprising exception: he hated
T.S. Eliot (whom he never
Met) and went out of his way
To broadcast his antipathy.
What Bill wrote about Eliot
Sounds now like a paranoid
Obsession. Bill saw Eliot as
A traitor who had left his
Country and its culture to go
Over to the British. To sense
The depth of Bill's rage we
Must try to understand how he
Felt, how some other American
Poets felt, when *The Waste Land*
Was published in 1922 with a
Success that carried all before
It. The literary landscape was
Altered overnight, obliterating,
Bill felt, the importance of
His own experimental work.

Since 1913 Bill had been feeling
His way, struggling, toward an
American idiom for poetry, a
Style built from American speech
And the sense of American locality.
The powerful impact of Eliot's
Anglo-Francophile verse bowled
Him over. The letter to Pound
At right, which mixes bitterness
With venom, may have been
Written in 1940.

From the *Autobiography*

"*The Waste Land* . . . wiped out our
world as if an atom bomb had been
dropped upon it and our brave sallies
into the unknown were turned to
dust.
    To me especially it struck like a
sardonic bullet. I felt at once that it
had set me back twenty years. . . .
Critically Eliot returned us to the
classroom just at the moment when
I felt that we were on the point of an
escape to matters much closer to the
essence of a new art form itself—
rooted in the locality which should
give it fruit . . . "

From a letter from Williams to Pound

"I'm glad you like Eliot's verse, but
I'm warning you, the only reason it
doesn't smell is that it's synthetic.
Maybe I'm wrong, but I distrust that
bastard more than any writer I know
in the world today. He can write,
granted, but it's like walking into a
church to me. I can't do it without a
bad feeling at the pit of my stomach.
Nothing has been learned there
since the simplicities were prevented
from becoming multiform by arrest-
ed growth. Bird'seye foods, suddenly
frozen at fifty degrees below zero,
under pressure, at perfect maturity,
immediately after being picked from
the can. It's pathological with me
perhaps, I hope not, but I am infuriated by such things. I am infuriated
because the arrest has taken place,
just at the point of risk, just at the

155

point where the magnificence might possibly have happened, just when the danger threatened, when the tradition might have led to the difficult new things. But the God damn liars prefer popes, prefer order, prefer freezing, prefer if you use the image,'the sterilization of the Christ they profess.' And the result is canned to make literature, with all the flavor, with all the pomp, while the real thing rots under their noses and they duck to the other side of the street. I despise and detest them. They are moles on a pig's belly instead of tits. Christ, how I hate their guts and the more so because Eliot, like his monumental wooden throne on wheels, that he carries around with him to worship, Eliot takes the place of the realizable actual, which is that much held back from realization precisely, of existence."

From *I Wanted to Write a Poem*

"I had known always that I wanted to write a long poem but I didn't know what I wanted to do until I got the idea of a man identified with a city. . . . What city?. . . I'd known about Paterson, even written about it. Suddenly it dawned on me I had a find. The Falls were spectacular; the river was a symbol handed to me. . . . This was my river and I was going to use it. I had grown up on its banks . . . "

With the passage of time, as
Bill's poetic reputation grew,
As the literary and academic
Worlds began to accept his
Concept of an "American idiom"
For poetry, he calmed down
About Eliot. But he had hurt
Himself in England. It took me
Twenty years to find a London
Publisher who would take on
His books, and in the end it
Was a firm set up by Granada
Films that took the risk, not
One of the old-line publishers.
And when Robert Lowell, still
Later, tried to bring about
A reconciliation, his efforts
Were not successful.

As the successive volumes of
Pound's *Cantos* were published
By New Directions, with praise
Taking the place of ridicule
And incomprehension, the idea
Grew in Bill's mind that he too
Should be at work on a long poem,
A "personal epic" as the *Cantos*
Were coming to be known. Fair
Enough, the friendly rivalry of
College days would continue.
But what kind of a poem should
It be? Obviously nothing like
The *Cantos*, either in content
Or technique. The *Cantos* were
International, ranging through

Every culture except that of
Latin America. But Bill's poem
Must be as American as the idiom
In which it would be written.
It would be New Jersey American
And its name would be *Paterson*,
The city near which he had been
Born and whose people he knew
So well from his doctoring.
For his symbol Bill took the
Passaic River as it follows its
Course down to the sea. He felt
That his life was like that
Of the river. At first he
Worried about the verse,
Then let the form take
Care of itself, permitting
Colloquial language to set the
Pace, flowing as easily as
The river flowed. He called his
Protagonist "Dr. Paterson," but
When he spoke of *Paterson* he
Meant both the man and the city.
They were the same. Yet for
The structure of the poem they
Had complementary identities.
Paterson was conceived, but
So much detailing remained
To be worked out. It became
Almost a lifework. The first
Notes for the poem in the
Williams archive at Buffalo
Date from 1926. The first
Volume appeared in 1946, the
Second in 1948, the third in

Author's Note to *Paterson Part I*

This is the first part of a long poem
in four parts—that a man himself is
a city, beginning, seeking, achieving
and concluding his life in ways
which the various aspects of a city
may embody—if imaginatively
conceived—any city, all the details
of which may be made to voice his
most intimate convictions. Part
One introduces the elemental character of the place. The Second Part
will comprise the modern replicas.
Three will seek a language to make
them vocal, and Four, the river
below the falls, will be reminiscent
of episodes—all that one man may
achieve in a lifetime.

Letter from WCW to JL, 1943

"That God damned and I mean God damned poem 'Paterson' has me down. I am burned up to do it but don't quite know how. I write and destroy, write and destroy. It's all shaped up in outline and intent, the body of the thinking is finished, but the technique, the manner and the method are unresolvable to date. I flounder and flunk."

And another in November 1948

"I get moments of despair over it, the usual thing, a feeling that I'm through for life, just a wash-out. Something lower than the lowest. Then again I spark along for a few lines and think I'm a genius. The usual crap. I'll do the best I can."

See the sample page from *Paterson (Book One)*, at right. Note the emphasis obtained by the extra vertical spacing around "unfledged" and "Divorce!" Note how the wide spacing of the dots after the first and fourth paragraphs extends the breath pauses. The heavily indented three words would not have been found in poems of a decade earlier. The omission of page numbers causes the type blocks to float on the page as if this were a drawing. Is there a bit of literary history in this layout, the prototype of the kind of free verse we practice now as a matter of course, and of the structure which Denise Levertov calls "organic form"?

1949, the fourth in 1951, and
The fifth in 1958. Bill often
Used to say, "This is the last
Of *Paterson*, Jim," but it wasn't
And in 1963 after he died we
Found notes for more pages. It
Might have gone on a long time
Further, partly because Bill
Agonized so much about it and was
Churned by such self-doubt. He
Often felt he had not found
The needed cohesive threads
For the work, and that his
Great poem, a whole life of
Writing, thought, and vision,
Was inevitably a failure.
At left is a letter he wrote
To me in December of 1943.

One problem in the publication
Of *Paterson* was to devise a
Distinctive typographical
Format for the text pages of
The book. For his early poems
Bill used a conventional page
Layout: a fixed left margin
Without indentations, regular
Vertical spacings, no half
Lines, few eccentricities in
Deployment. It was tame-cat
Layout, nothing modern
About it. For *Paterson* he
Wanted something far more
Visual and expressive. Broken
Lines, short lines mixed with

158

on a log, her varnished hair
trussed up like a termite's nest (forming
the lines) and, her old thighs
gripping the log reverently, that,
all of a piece, holds up the others—
alert: begin to know the mottled branch
that sings .

certainly NOT the university,
a green bud fallen upon the pavement its
sweet breath suppressed: Divorce (the
language stutters)

unfledged:

two sisters from whose open mouths
Easter is born—crying aloud,

Divorce!

While
the green bush sways: is whence
I draw my breath, swaying, all of a piece,
separate, livens briefly, for the moment
unafraid   .   .

Which is to say, though it be poorly
said, there is a first wife
and a first beauty, complex, ovate—
the woody sepals standing back under
the stress to hold it there, innate

PATERSON

(BOOK ONE)

A NEW
DIREC-
TIONS
BOOK

WILLIAM CARLOS
WILLIAMS

Long lines, variations in
Vertical spacing, in short
A page where the type would
Float free, as unrestrained as
The ideas the words were stating.
He wanted to liberate the words
And lines on the page. Bill had
A strong visual sense. As a young
Man he had done some creditable
Painting. From the days of the
Armory Show of 1913 he had been
Interested in painting and had
Close painter friends. From his
Trips to Europe he knew what
Apollinaire had done with his
Calligrammes and how the Dadaists
And Surrealists had experimented
With typography. It was only
Natural that he should conceive
Of a page of type as a free-form
Design. When I showed Bill's
Script to our salesman at Haddon
Craftsmen, the commercial printer
New Directions often used, he
Said that such composition
Would cost an arm and a leg;
The irregular spacing couldn't
Be done by linotype. By luck I
Had heard of a small printer,
George W. Van Vechten in
Metuchen, New Jersey, who
Enjoyed solving typographical
Problems in books. Bill and
Van Vechten took to each other.

160

The compositor sensed at once
The forms that the poet was
Groping for, and gave him many
Proofs set in various ways to
Choose from. I wish I'd urged
Bill to dedicate *Paterson* to
George. This was a case where
An intuitive designer helped
Perfect a great work.

Pound's *Cantos* are immersed
In quotations or concealed
Or erroneous references. I
Remember watching him work
In Rapallo when he was too
Excited to check his sources.
He was content to paraphrase
Or to insert in his line
A suggestive, brief phrase.
With Bill it was different.
He wanted specificity and
Accuracy in the quotations.
The early pages of *Paterson*
Are loaded with passages from
Old newspapers and histories
Of the region. And these are
Verbatim, not the poet's
Reconstruction of the events
As Pound would have done it.
So it was up to Van Vechten
To find graceful treatments of
Such interpolations. These
Alternations of prose with
Verse were one of the, to many

Readers, startling innovations
Of the poem. It's true that
His early *Spring and All* mixed
Prose and verse but that was in
1923 in a book which almost no
One saw. For Bill prose and verse
Were the same thing, as he
Expounded to Parker Tyler in
The letter of 1948, at left:
A novelty in the prose-poetry
Structure of *Paterson* was the
Inclusion of a number of verbatim
Texts of letters which friends
And acquaintances had written
To Bill. Their content had no
Relation to that of the poem.
Why were these people there?
I suppose they were peripheral
Elements in the grand mosaic
Of the work. In *I Wanted to
Write a Poem* of 1958 Bill had
Said: "I used documentary
Prose to break up the poetry,
To help shape the form of the
Poem....The poetic and the anti-
Poetic are all one piece."
Letters were from such as Pound
And the poet Richard Eberhart,
The novelist Josephine Herbst
And an adoring Rutherford
Neighbor, Kitty Hoagland, who
Often helped Bill out when
There were booklength scripts
To be typed; "Dreadful Edward"

From WCW to Parker Tyler, 1948

"All the prose, including the tail which would have liked to have wagged the dog, has primarily the purpose of giving a metrical meaning to or of emphasizing a metrical continuity between all word use. It is *not* an antipoetic device, the repeating of which piece of miscalculation makes me want to puke. It *is* that prose and verse are both *writing*, both a matter of the words and an interrelation between words for the purpose of exposition, or other better defined purpose of *the art*. Please do not stress other 'meanings.' I want to say that prose and verse are to me the same thing, that verse (as in Chaucer's tales) belongs *with* prose, as the poet belongs with 'Mine host,' who says in so many words to Chaucer, 'Namoor, all that rhyming is not worth a toord.' Poetry does not *have* to be kept away from prose as Mr. Eliot might insist, it goes *along with* prose and, companionably, it itself, without aid or excuse or need for separation or bolstering, shows itself by *itself* for what it is. It *belongs* there, in the gutter. Not anywhere else or whatever it is the same: the poem."

162

Dahlberg, the most disagreeable
Author New Directions ever
Published (but *Because I Was
Flesh*, his autobiography, is a
Masterpiece); Gil Sorrentino,
Now an eminent avant-garde
Novelist; the enigmatic poet
Marcia Nardi; Allen Ginsberg
Who had grown up in Paterson.
(Allen persists in denying my
Anecdote that he became Bill's
Friend by leaving his poems
In the Williams's milk bottles,
But some myths are too good,
Too mythic to be suppressed.)

Marcia Nardi, impoverished
And embittered to the point
Of paranoia, living alone in
A shack in the woods near
Woodstock, was not for Bill
A romantic attachment. She
Was the symbol of woman
Victimized in a male society.
Her long letters inserted in
Paterson (one is eight full
Pages) insisting on having
Bill recognize her work and
Urging him to help her
Get it published, these pages
Expand her to a major female
Character till she becomes
As it were the figurative
Heroine of the epic. In the

Spring and All

by

William Carlos Williams

Text Bill signed her letters
"Cress," the reference being
To Shakespeare's *Cressida*.
The letters had more interest
For him than Nardi's verse,
Giving a social dimension
That the poem had lacked.
He called them "some of the
Best writing by a woman (or
By anyone else) I have seen
In years," and in one of his
Replies he tells her:

As he so often did when he
Wanted to encourage a young
Poet, Bill prevailed on me to
Put a group of Nardi's poems
In our New Directions annual.
I dragged my feet a bit—I
Found her work squishy—but
He insisted. At left are a few
Lines of typical Nardi; they
Are inferior to her letters.
Yet her letters give *Paterson*
A female contrapuntal voice
In the midst of so much that is
Masculine. Nardi's letters
Became structurally important
For Bill; when he finished
Book Two and imagined that was
The end of the poem, for his
Coda he chose not a passage of
Verse but the longest of Nardi's
Letters, one that summarized
Her position in their exchange.

Excerpt from a letter to Nardi

"Your letters show you to have one
of the best minds I have ever
encountered. I say nothing of its
reach which I have had no
opportunity to measure but its
truth and strength. Your words as I
read them have a vigor and cleanli-
ness to them which constitute for
me real beauty. I sincerely and
deeply admire you."

From poems by Marcia Nardi

The mind and flesh embrace
        each other.
Words yearning like breasts
        within a brain of stone—
Thought's fine perceptions
        thickening to press
A cageless mirrored body
        to her own.

From a Marcia Nardi letter

"My attitude toward woman's
wretched position in society and
my ideas about all the changes necessary there, were interesting to you
weren't they, in so far as they made
for *literature*? . . . And you saw in
one of my first letters to you . . . that
my thoughts were to be taken seriously, because that too could be
turned by you into literature, as
something disconnected from life."

164

Over the years the sending of
Poems dwindled considerably
But Bill was able to get some
Small grants for Nardi and a
Book of her poems was brought
Out by Black Sparrow Press in
1956. A study of her work by
Elizabeth O'Neil will soon be
Published. She died in 1990.

As *Paterson* first took shape
In Bill's mind the name of his
Persona was simply "Dr. Paterson."
But as its scope was expanded
He became "Noah Faitout Paterson";
"Noah" was for surviving the
Flood of words that had threatened
To drown him. "Faitout" was in
Honor of Bill's friend David
Lyle, Rutherford's omnididact,
Who could do anything and was
As *polumetis* as Odysseus: the
Man of many skills and endless
Devisings. "Dr. Noah Faitout
Paterson": he could do it all.

In the *Cantos* Pound is his own
Protagonist. He puts down in the
Poem everything that has touched
His life in any way: every culture,
Every human connection; everything
He has read, seen or heard. These
Are his "phalanx of particulars."
Williams's protagonist covers less
Ground. "Dr. Paterson," wandering

Through the city, for the most
Part limits his range to the
Local, the environs of Paterson,
The people of New Jersey. But in
A sense as deep as with Pound
Language is the underlying subject
Of *Paterson*, even the motif of the
Poem if you will. The key phrase
Which is repeated several times
In the text is "the search for
A redeeming language." Near the
Beginning, referring to those
Whose lives have little meaning,
Bill writes:

"The language, the language
         fails them
They do not know the words
         or have not
The courage to use them ."

Is "the language" a higher power,
More fundamental to him than
The oft repeated "no ideas but in
Things," which he borrowed from
The "*nihil in intellectu quod non
Prius in sensu*" of Scholasticism?

Despite the great pressures on
Him of having two intensive
Careers, his medical practice
And the writing of one book after
Another, being friends with Bill
Was, on the whole, happy sailing,

✴

THE
COMPLETE
COLLECTED POEMS OF
WILLIAM CARLOS
WILLIAMS
1906-1938
✴

New Directions : Norfolk, Connecticut

166

Up at least till the calamity of
David McDowell's intrigue. Bill
Had his moods, of course, but
Basically he was even-tempered,
With a good sense of humor, and
Ready to overlook my mistakes
And shortcomings as a publisher.
The actual amount of time we were
Able to spend together was not
Great. When I was finishing up
At Harvard, I didn't get my
Diploma until the end of term
In 1939, the trip down to see
Him in Rutherford was long by
Car. No planes then. Later when
I was running both New Directions
And the ski resort in Utah my
Visits were more infrequent.
But there were exceptions such
As the summer when my aunt made
Floss and Bill the loan of her
Mountaintop cottage in Norfolk,
Where we had good talks and
Walks in the forest. A rest was
What Floss and Bill wanted. I
Saw that they got it. I fetched
Their groceries from the village
While my aunt kept the local
Literary folk at bay. Another
Good get-together was a trip
With Bill to Charlottesville
Where the University was the
Sponsor of a conference on
Douglasite Social Credit. Pound

In his letters was constantly
Badgering Bill about monetary
Reforms, how it wasn't right
For banks to "create money" by
The issuance of credit, a power
Which belonged only to Congress
As set forth in the Constitution.
Douglas's twin theories of the
National Dividend and the Just
Price appealed to Bill because
He knew from the doctoring in
Poor communities that much was
Amiss in the social–economic
Order. His poems are tinged
Often with deep social concern.
A strain of social archaeology
Runs through *Paterson*. Bill's
Prose book *In the American Grain*
Looks at our history from
Red Eric to Lincoln to show how
We became what we are today as
Americans. But Bill never got
On the bandwagon of proletarian
Writing. He didn't let leftist
Friends such as Louis Zukofsky
Or Fred Miller push him into
Communism. I never thought of
Him as "political." I saw him
As humanitarian and libertarian.
Perhaps his only "political"
Poem is the famous "To Elsie,"
Which begins: "The pure products
Of America go crazy…" At the
University of Virginia conference

His talk was a moving statement
On "Social Credit as Anti-Communism."
He landed some good punches on
The bankers, but how many took
Him seriously? Bankers are as
Sacred as Baptist preachers. In
Book IV, Part II of *Paterson* Bill
Gave a full page to a Social
Credit tract announcing that
"The Constitution says: To borrow
Money on the credit of the United
States. It does not say: To borrow
Money from pirate bankers."

What was Bill really like? Have
I come anywhere near catching
Him as he was? Probably not. His
Nature was complicated, though
It did not seem so on a first
Meeting. Then he was all charm.
A spontaneous charm so that one
Didn't have the feeling of being
Intentionally charmed. Inner
Conflicts were at first hidden
Under the surface, attitudes
That ranged from the puritan to
The bohemian. His was not a
Disciplined disposition, any
More than his poems were. His
Personality floated free, it
Was governed by changing moods.
Herbert Leibowitz has written
Of Bill's character that it was
Full of "volatile cross-purposes."

The Farmers' Daughters
The Collected Stories of
William Carlos Williams

169

Bill was generous, a giver of
Himself, but there were times
When he could suddenly turn
Brusque or indifferent. It
Occurred to me once, seeing
This happen, that the idea
For a poem had come into his
Head and it was more important
To him to work it out than to
Carry on the conversation. Bill
Could drift off for a while
And then return as if he had
Finished the poem, which he
Would then jot down on one
Of his medical prescription
Slips (hundreds of these are
Preserved in the Yale library
Archive). Bill's mind was of
Many layers. Some of them he
Seemed to want to conceal. He
Could shift quickly from a
Comic mood that was almost
Manic to a look and tone that
Suggested the bitterness of
Depression. But such episodes
Were brief, though once in
1952, following one of the
Strokes that plagued his later
Years he felt it necessary to
Commit himself for treatment
In a sanitarium. His adviser
In such matters was the Boston
Poet-psychiatrist Merrill Moore,
The man who is said to have
Written fifty thousand sonnets.

Could there have been a genetic
Flaw that Bill inherited from
His mother, Elena Hoheb, partly
French from Martinique, partly
Dutch-Spanish-Jewish? No, that's
Far-fetched. Yet I remember her
As having a force of temperament
That went beyond eccentricity.
Bill was devoted to this tiny
Woman who had grown up in Puerto
Rico and Paris. When she came
To live at 9 Ridge Road and then
Became feeble he carried her up
And down stairs. He wrote a
Book about her, *Yes, Mrs. Williams*,
A reminiscence in which he put
Down her life as a girl and young
Woman in the islands and in Paris,
As she told it to him in a mixture
Of French, Spanish, and English.
She died at the age of 102.

Of course the most understanding
Historian of Bill is his son
Dr. William Eric, who lives at
9 Ridge Road and had his office
There, a pediatrician like his
Father, until he recently retired.
*"Flossy, The Physical, Upbringing,
My Father the Doctor, Money, The
House, Food, Cars…"* these are
Some of the chapter titles for
The memoir that Bill Junior is
Writing about his dad. Here is
A scene that he remembers:

"It was at night that Dad would call on apparently endless stores of energy, the tattoo of his typewriter providing a reassuring lullaby to which my brother Paul and I slept and awoke throughout childhood. I can recall the projection of his mood brought to me by the cadence of the keys—the smooth andante when all was happy and serene, and the interrupted staccato when the going got rough, the carriage slamming, and the paper ripped from the roller, balled, and heaved in the direction of the wastebasket. Night was his time to roar. Here was happiness, his love, Poetry . . . "

And his description of his dad:

"He was about five feet nine inches tall, shoe size 8D, hat size 7 1/4, shirt size 15 1/2–32, waist 32 to 34, with good posture in both standing and sitting positions. His weight fluctuated between 150 and 160 pounds and was well distributed. . . . His gait was purposeful. You felt he had a goal in mind as he strode along. . . . His hands were spadelike, a ditch-digger's, he used to say, with blunt-tipped fingers and calloused palms. He was always clean shaven. . . . The unruly jet black hair epitomized in his self-portrait gradually gave way to baldness and an encircling halo of gray at the periphery of his skull. His eyes were dark brown, always searching, looking not only at you but into you, not impolitely but in an interested kind of way. There was nothing distinguished about his mouth. His dominating facial feature of course was his nose, which he recognized and early on glorified in his own poem 'Smell!'

> "Oh strong-ridged and deeply hollowed
> nose of mine! what will you not be smelling?
> . . .
> Must you taste everything? Must you know
> everything?
> Must you have a part in everything?"

He had a weathered skin of slightly olive hue. He and his
father and brother Edgar walked hundreds of miles for the fun
of it. . . . He would take a trolley out of town 8 or 10 miles
and then walk home. His sleep requirement was minimal. . . .
He needed physical work for an outlet, and there was about
him an aura of tension, an invisible halo of potential that
demanded a constant outlet. Yet he remained approachable.
There was nothing obtrusive in his manner. People seemed
to sense that here was a nice guy, who far from being
offended, welcomed human contact."

The break, which happily was not
Permanent, between Bill and myself
Was not the fault or the intention
Of either one of us. It was the
Result of an intrigue engineered
By a meddlesome, self-serving rogue,
Now deceased, named David McDowell,
Whom I had hired in 1948 to help
Me run the sales and promotion side
Of New Directions. In his way Dave
Was brilliant as a sales manager;
If he had stuck to the job for which
He had been taken on all would have
Been well. The office crew liked him
And with his Southern charm, he
Was from Tennessee, he made a
Good impression for the firm
With reviewers and bookstore
People. His problem was that he
Was ambitious to the point of
Obsession. He wanted to get ahead,
He wanted power and money at
Any cost, morality be damned.
When David found that I was

Spending much time out in Utah
At the ski resort at Alta,
Which I was developing, he
Saw an opportunity to try to
Take control of New Directions.
Surreptitiously he began to
Cultivate certain ND authors,
Inviting them to lunch on the
Office expense account, but
Worse than this, he started to
Solicit manuscripts on his own
From other writers and from
Second-raters at that, people
Whose work I would never think
Of accepting. When I found out
I naturally gave him the bounce.
And from the nonchalant way he
Took it, I should have guessed
He had a larger plan in mind,
To wit, the alienation of Bill
From me and New Directions,
To whisk him away to another
Publisher. Which, precisely,
Was what happened. David rented
A house in Rutherford for his
Wife and himself, and he set
Out to pay court by making
Himself useful to Bill and
Subverting Bill's loyalty to
Me and New Directions. He told
Bill that our distribution was
Bad and that I was too tight to
Spend much money on advertising.
The latter is true; publishers

Know to their pain that highbrow
Literary books can't be sold by
Ads, only good reviews and word
Of mouth will sell them. As for
Distribution that depends on the
Enthusiasm of the salesmen. Ours
Loved our books and always did
A good job. Bill had never been
Concerned about these matters
Though he did chide me about my
Giving so much time to the ski-
Lift business. He had reached a
Stage in his career when he
Wondered why he was not as famous
As Pound or Stevens. And he
Also worried about what Floss
Would live on after his death.
These anxieties made him fertile
Ground for McDowell's plotting.
That one, that Iago, made his
Next move by approaching the
President of Random House, that
Renowned editor of joke books,
Mr. Bennett Cerf, who readily
Took the bait, promising Iago
A job if he could come bearing
A three-book contract with Bill.
In short order Bill had become
A Random House author and, with
The help of his new editor,
Began assembling *Make Light of
It*, the collection of stories
That appeared in 1950. And so
Commenced the winter of my

Discontent that lasted eight
Years. The letters exchanged
Then, Bill's benign but adamant,
Mine awash with desperation and
Anguish, make painful reading
Now, but I guess they are part
Of literary history and should
At least be quoted from:

Bill to Jim, February 9, 1950:

I think I'll have a talk with McDowell now that he's with
Random House for I tell you frankly I'm not satisfied to let
things run on the way they've been going.

It isn't that I've not been satisfied with our arrangements
in the past. . . . It's the future I have to think of. . . . So, if
you'll agree, I'd like to limit ourselves to this: That you bring
out, now, the *Collected Poems* as you have planned them and
Paterson IV just as soon as I can complete it, everything else
to be crossed off the list.

By this I shall gain a free hand to try myself out, to see just
how far I can go with sales. . . . I'll never make any real cash
through you. Nor have I wanted it until now when either I
must get on with medicine or somehow or other get me
more income by writing, one or the other.

Jim to Bill, February 12, 1950:

Yours of the 9th to hand, and what a magnificent kick in the
teeth that is—administered, I may say, with a touch that is
definitely deft, and almost that, one might think, of a prac-
ticed hand at this sort of thing; which, of course, you aren't—
the furthest thing from it—but how easily we drift into it
when the devil has planted the seed.

Yes, a lovely reward for a decade of work and faith and sacrifice. More power to you. I love the human race. The more they try to kick me around the better I love them. Sure thing.

Frankly, Bill, I would never have dreamt that you, of all people, would fall this low. I suppose I have always carried you around on my special idealistic pedestal. You have always seemed to me the whitest of the white, the real human being—complete with sense and feeling.

Well, I am hurt. I am terribly hurt, I won't conceal it, and from the quarter I most trusted. A hundred times when other publishers have told me what faithless bastards writers are I have held you up as an example of loyalty. I feel exactly like Gretchen's brother in Faust. Look up the passage and read it for me.

But go your way—with my blessing. You are a loveable cuss, and I'll be sore for a few weeks, but it will pass. What you are doing is only human, and I've done plenty of things myself on a par with it. I can't complain.

Still in all, it's incredible, unbelievable. Have you no insight? Are you totally blind about your work and its nature? Do you really think that you can sell yourself to the masses, no matter how hard you try to write what they want?

All right . . . go to the big boys. They were swell to you about publishing *White Mule*, weren't they? They did a beautiful job on the *Collected Poems* didn't they? They fell over themselves didn't they to get a critic to write a book about you? They overwhelmed you, didn't they, with offers to keep the *American Grain* in print? Go to them. Rush. Run. Don't lose a second. Let them slobber their dirt all over your decency and your purity. And offer up to them as a little bribe *my* pride, and my life's devotion to an ideal. See how dirty they can make that too.

. . .

Well Bill, I'm sorry to have talked to you this way. It's not respectful, it's not friendly. But you have hurt me deeply and terribly, and the only way to get it out of my system is to talk right out, cauterize it, and then forget it.

You say you need money. Let me remind you that I offered to put you on a monthly check basis, as I do with [Henry] Miller, and you turned it down. I suppose you had your reasons.

Bill to Jim, March 9, 1950

I've made up my mind and having done so I write to you at once that you may know how we stand. I want you to do my poems as you have done in the past but my prose will go to someone else, probably Random House, under McDowell's editorship. This may prove somewhat of a wrench to both of us but there's no escaping it.

This chance has got to be taken if I'm to go on as a writer. For I can't make any money with you and I've got to try to earn at least a partial living by writing.

With this settled in my own mind I'm getting the new, two volume *Collected* in order for Kaplan; it'll take me a few weeks to do it. The short stories, before I give them to McDowell, I shall hold for two weeks or until I can hear from you.

I hope this will satisfy you and that you will give the deal your blessing but it is final.

What respect I might ever
Have had for David McDowell
Was blown away when his next
Fandango came to light a few
Weeks after he had moved
To Random House. This was
The story. One morning at
The New Directions office I

Wanted to check a point
In the manuscript of a book
We were publishing, a work
By a leading author. I kept
The manuscript in our safe.
But when I opened the safe
The manuscript was nowhere
To be found. I searched the
Shelves; it wasn't there.
Only two of us could work
That combination, I myself
And McDowell. What must have
Happened is obvious. He had
Taken his keys—his office
Keys and those to the building
—To a hardware store and had
Had them copied before he
Turned them in, then he had
Come up the fire stairs, which
Were open at night. Rare book
Dealers in the city would jump
At the chance to buy such a
Valuable manuscript and they
Wouldn't ask any questions
Either. Of course the police
Showed up. They investigated.
But nothing ever came of it:
They really had no evidence
Of a crime without an eye-
Witness or recovery of the
Loot and they couldn't press
Charges. The thief was clear,
He had pulled off his revenge.
Where is the manuscript now?

In the hands of a private
Collector perhaps. In Texas?
England? Tokyo? Who knows?
Well, I had invoked Apollo,
God of the lyre, and also
Hermes, he who created the
Lyre from a tortoise shell,
To put a curse on McDowell.
They did. But they took their
Own sweet time about it. "Like
A green bay tree in springtime
The wicked shall flourish"—
So Cicero remarked somewhere.
(But I've forgotten the Latin.)
I made no effort to keep tabs
On McDowell. I just wanted to
Forget about him. I should have
Spotted him as a lemon and not
Hired him. Luckily I found a
Wonderful replacement before
Long in Bob MacGregor. Bob
Became the managing director
Of New Directions and ran it
Far better than I could have
For twenty years. He assumed
Complete charge in 1952 when I
Took leave to run Intercultural
Publications, a branch of the
Ford Foundation, which had me
Working most of my time abroad
In Europe and Asia. This was
An exciting change for me, I
Might be in Paris one day and
New Delhi the next, which kept
Me from dwelling on McDowell's

Rascality. He lasted only five
Years with Random House, where
He put out a Williams book each
Year, but Bill's books didn't
Sell much better with the big
Firm than they had with New
Directions. Predictably the
Romance with Cerf cooled off.
McDowell then found a friend,
A stockbroker, to back him in
His own company, but this was
A failure. He began to drink
Heavily and his nice little
Italian wife left him, taking
The children with her. After
That I heard of various short
Stints with other firms, but
Apparently the drink took over
And in time he went back to
Tennessee to an early death.

Life in the timeless East
Conduces to thought. In
Rangoon where with the help
Of U Thant, who was running
Burma for his mystical friend
U Nu, I was assembling a
Perspectives of Burma, I had
Some instruction in meditation
From a wonderful lady named
Daw Khin Myo Chit. It was far
From instantaneous but I came
To see that the break with
Bill was pretty much my fault.
It had been wrong for me to

IMAGINATIONS
William Carlos Williams
Kora in Hell / Spring and All / The Descent of Winter
The Great American Novel / A Novelette & Other Prose

Spend so much time building
Ski lifts when my important
Work in life was to promote
The books of great poets. I
Determined somehow to make a
Mea culpa when I got back to
The States for good. Bill made
This easy for me by his own
Admission. He wrote me that
He realized that McDowell had
Used him and that he never
Wanted to see the man again.
He sent me the manuscript of
Part V of *Paterson*, declaring
His hope that we would be
Working together for the rest
Of his life. And so it was:
The Farmers' Daughters (the
Collected stories) in 1961,
Many Loves (the collected
Plays) in the same year, and
The last book of poems,
Pictures from Brueghel, which
Won a posthumous Pulitzer
Prize. Someone had given Bill
An album of Peter Brueghel
Paintings which he studied
Lovingly when his eyes were
Too tired to read print. These
Small descriptive poems are
Among his finest, glimpses
Into a past which he made
Contemporary in his vision.

Bill had taken me back, but
I still wanted to make my
Mea culpa to him. It must
Be formal, be in writing. It
Came to me that it should be
Done fictionally, and so
We have my story "A Visit,"
Which I published first in the
*William Carlos Williams News-
Letter* and then reprinted it
In my book *Random Stories*.

A young publisher, Marshall
MacDonald, drives out from
The city to make his apology
To an elderly lawyer, Homer
Evans, who has suffered a
Stroke and had difficulty in
Finding his words. Driving
To Rutherford, MacDonald
Remembers many things about
Evans, but once there he is
So absorbed in his friend's
Conversation that he forgets
His mission and must return to
Complete it. Now as I reread
This story I find passages so
Right about Bill that I want
To quote them, even at the
Risk of repeating myself:
(The "he" is MacDonald, i.e.
JL. "Evans" of course is Bill.
The scene is at 9 Ridge Road).

Something to Say

William Carlos Williams on Younger Poets

EDITED BY JAMES E. B. BRESLIN

As he moved about the living room, taking it in, he heard a noise from upstairs that he couldn't at first identify. It was a series of regular, repeated sounds—first a kind of soft scrape and then a little thump . . . then another scrape and thump. Suddenly it struck him; Evans must be dragging himself downstairs, holding onto the bannister and dragging one leg that had lost its mobility. It had gotten to that, the poor man could hardly walk anymore!

. . .

. . . Evans looked older and his hair, what there was of it, was white, but his figure was erect and his face ruddy and little lined for a man in his late seventies. He was wearing spectacles with much thicker lenses—the last bout in the hospital had been an operation for cataracts—but the magnifying effect of the glasses made his eyes appear even more lively than usual.

Evans had wonderful eyes. People remembered his eyes. He had always been rather handsome in a crisp, lean-faced, eager-looking way, but his eyes—brown with a dancing light in them, a merriment in them—were the dominant feature. He could never have been much of a poker player with such expressive eyes. Every movement from a mind that was constantly in motion came through them. And now the magnification of the lenses brought this play of feeling even closer to the person near him.

. . .

In his poetry and in the essays—those "Letters from Nowhere" with which he had peppered the magazines for years, having his say in freewheeling style about anything that caught his eye or crossed his mind, from the new book by a young unknown to the probable effect of syphilis on Beethoven's music, Evans had always been as unrestrained in language, as unconcerned with taboos, as the newest would-be Rimbaud in the Village or North Beach. He had kept young with the youngest, and this had been a part of his appeal to successive generations. He didn't date. In his writing there was neither pontification or withdrawal to a protected height. At seventy he could still be playful, at times a little ingenuous.

. . .

With Evans creation was a matter of spontaneous (and sometimes almost continuous) combustion. Even on weekends he seldom had time to sit down to write with an open space of a whole morning before him. He had to catch the sparks as they flew. And how they flew! It was as if he were under a rain of cosmic rays, invisible pellets that showered him from God knew where, leaving marks on the sensitive plate in his mind which were immediately translated into images made of words. And the greater the pressure of law work, the more intense the bombardment. On vacations, when he did have free time, he wrote less than during the crowded rest of the year.

This way of writing had certainly influenced his style. With ellipses and leaps from image to image it was almost a poetic shorthand. There was something skeletal about his poems, even the long ones. Evans had no time to hammer out ornamentation, or to fashion much flesh between the bones. Part of the power of his poetry was in its very rawness, the fresh bite of the perception coming through to the reader as directly as it had to the poet in the simple, uncluttered phrasing. Of course, there was an elegance too; a man with an ear doesn't work with words fifty years for nothing. And it was not automatic writing; Evans did revise and rework. In the evenings, or on weekends, he would tinker with the sheets of drafts, trying different sequences and combinations. But he had never won the good opinion of the professor-critics for whom a poet must be as intricate as a complicated machine. Evans' work was not a happy hunting ground for the exegetes. An Evans poem said what it had to say at first reading. It offered no temptation to the academic maggots.

The force of this life that had put together two such

different impulses—the down-to-earth setting things in order of homely law work and the wild escape into free imagination, into a kind of intentional dis-ordering, of poetry—came across to MacDonald as he sat close to Evans, more or less silently studying him as the old man searched for and found his words. A frail but electric man who all his life had had command of words, could summon them instantly to his use, and now, like the nightmare of a runner who cannot move his legs in his bad dream, a very nasty joke of fate, had to fight to bring them from his brain to his tongue. MacDonald could see how this injustice hurt Evans' pride. The poet became silent and began to look at his hands, rubbing one with the other. The hands were the only part of him which really betrayed his age. They were mottled with dark spots of brown and some of the veins stood up like blue vines on the skin.

. . .

". . . these kids, these new young poets, they know what they've got to do and they're going on with it. I don't want them to copy me you understand. I give them hell when they're just doing what I did. They've got to go further with it. I don't know if I ever really made it a metric. But what is metric anyway? I read all the books about it once and I still don't know. But I know you've got to have it, it has to be there. It has to be speech and something else, too. It's nothing to do with scansion or tum-tee-tum but there has to be a base under the way the lines fall. I thought I had it the way I wanted it in 'Long Night,' I thought that was as far as I could go with it, but I'm not sure. I've still got more to do . . . and how am I going to do it now?

"Well, I keep after it. I'm still pretty good with my left." Evans held up his hands in front of him and looked at them, as if they belonged to somebody else. "This one is pretty well shot—the fingers won't do what I want them to anymore. But I can still type with my left. I peck it out—without the capitals, it's too slow to hunt for that shift—and then Helen

186

fixes it up for me. It still wants to come out. You'd think it
would quit when everything else is going but it's still there.
Some mornings it even wakes me up. I can't wait to get
dressed or eat my breakfast. But it takes so long now to work
it out. It's there and I know the words I want for it but I
don't have them. I just have to sit till they come out of that
fog in there. She can't help me on that. Sometimes it takes
the whole morning to work it out, just ten or twenty lines
in a whole morning—or I have to go back to it the next day.
. . .

"It's a funny thing that I can't quit. I sit here and take it
. . . and you know I've never been able to write about death.
I never had anything to say about it. All those poems and
almost nothing about death in any of them. I don't like it,
Marsh, I'm afraid of it. I have to rest a lot now but I don't
sleep much. I just have to lie there and face up to it—that
pretty soon now I'm not going to be around. That's just a lot
of shit about people being ready to die. And you know I've
never been able to get anywhere with the idea of anything
coming after. You go out like a light and you're out. I believe
that. I don't expect anything else. But this thing won't stop.
It's as strong now as it ever was, maybe stronger. And I don't
think it's just habit. Maybe it is, but I don't think so. It's like
there was somebody else in there. Look at me. I can hardly
talk, this is more than I've talked in six months. I'm ready to
fall apart, but this thing is at me just as hard as ever."

Halfway back to Manhattan
MacDonald becomes aware that
He has forgotten to tell Evans
About his remorse, which was
His purpose for the visit. He
Returns to 9 Ridge Road but
Finds Evans upstairs sleeping.
Fearful, he tells Helen he
Must see the old man anyway.

Evans raised himself on his pillows and snapped on the bedside table lamp. He was in his shirtsleeves with his tie off. He fumbled for his glasses on the table. MacDonald put them in his hand and sat down on the bed beside him. His words came tumbling out.

"I'm sorry to disturb you, but I forgot to tell you the most important thing, what I really came to see you for. You see I . . . I don't know just how to . . . well I have to make sure that you knew that I was sorry."

"Sorry? I don't see what..."

"About what happened between us. Only really it was what I did to you. I can understand that now and I wanted to tell you I was sorry I wrote those letters . . . and all the rest of it."

Evans was startled . . . . but then he took it all in and began to laugh. It wasn't a big laugh, but a little soft prolonged chuckle, and his head nodded from side to side as he pulled his good left hand out from beneath the blanket, felt for MacDonald's hand and covered it with his.

"Why, Marsh," he said, "you didn't have to come back here to tell me that. I knew that. I knew it when it happened. I knew you didn't mean all that stuff you wrote me."

"I guess I did mean it then. But I shouldn't have. And I don't now." He gave Evans' hand a squeeze and got up. "I'll get out of here now. I'm sorry I woke you up."

"You didn't," said Evans, "I was just lying here . . . thinking of . . . of . . . Venice, of all things." And as MacDonald left him, "But I'm glad you came back."

What I remember most about
Bill's strokes, there were
At least four of them, the
First in 1947, was his dogged
Courage in fighting back from

Them. He wouldn't give in. At
A certain point he had to
Cut back on his doctoring
And then give it up entirely,
But nothing could stop him
From writing, even when he
Had to type with only one
Finger and mis-hit many keys
Anyway. After one of
His strokes be could hardly
Speak for several months.
Memory for words was very
Poor, but he never asked me
Not to come out to see him
At 9 Ridge Road (he refused
To go into the hospital).

Having visitors was part of
His battle for recovery.
For me these visits were
Agonizing. I wanted to help him
With the word I knew he was
Struggling to remember, but
He wouldn't let me. He would
Fight with his memory till
The right word finally came
Into his head. What guts he
Had and how much strength,
Considering what he'd been
Through to keep up the
Fight when anyone else in
His condition would have
Given up. Floss read aloud
To him and helped him with
His mail. The sons, Bill Jr.
And Paul, stopped by as often
As they could to spell her.

After the first stroke when
He was in bed in the home of
Charles Abbott, the curator
Of poetry at the University
Of Buffalo (where many of his
Papers are now housed) I did
My bit fixing up the plays
That he hadn't completed for
The *Many Loves* collection.
Composing the directions for
Staging to go into the book
Was simply beyond his grasp;
I wrote all of them for *The*
Cure, which is not a good
Play. It is a metaphor of
His own desperate situation,
Being the story of a young
Poet who is knocked out of
His senses in a motorcycle
Accident and restored to
Life by the girl who nurses
Him. It can also be seen as
A trope of the restoration
Of creativity through love.

During the period of his
Strokes Bill very belatedly
Achieved fame, at least in
The academic world and among
Serious readers of poetry.
He was no longer the obscure
Pediatrician in Rutherford
Who wrote a nutty poem about
A red wheelbarrow and some
Chickens. Almost overnight

Bill emerged as a major poet,
Ranked with Pound and Stevens.
There were honorary degrees
And more invitations to do
Readings than he was well
Enough to fulfill. There
Were prizes and conferences.
The only setback came when
His appointment as Consultant
In Poetry at the Library of
Congress was slickly aborted.

To me one of the remarkable
Things about Bill's old age
Was his vision of what he
Called the "variable foot"
And his struggle to find it.
It was almost like an intense
Religious conversion, like
The pursuit of a metrical
Holy Grail. The exponent of
Free forms developed a need
For a traditional metric. I
Think it was a psychic need,
A throwback to his childhood
When his English-born
Father, William George, would
Read aloud (those were the days
Before radio and TV) almost all
Of Shakespeare, much Kipling
And endless verse from Palgrave's
Golden Treasury. When Bill began
To write his first substantial
Effort was an *Endymion* and next
In the 1909 pamphlet *Poems* it

Was wretched imitations of Keats,
Rhymed octosyllabic mush. (At
The end of his life Bill had me
Promise that none of this early
Trash would ever be reprinted.)
What extracted Bill from this
Drivel? Probably a combination
Of influences: reading Whitman,
Pound's sarcastic derision,
What he saw his contemporaries
Writing, Maxwell Bodenheim,
Mina Loy, the *Others* group
Led by Alfred Kreymborg, and
The poets in Harriet Monroe's
Poetry in Chicago. The work of
Avant-garde French painters
In the Armory Show of 1913, who
Were abandoning representation
In favor of abstraction, was
Important too. Soon Bill gave
Up rhyme and the tum-tee-tum
Meters. Within ten years he
Had perfected his own New
Jersey brand of *vers libre*,
As in "The Revelation" (1914):
He went on to become the best
Line-breaker of his time; i.e.
He had the most sensitive ear
For judging which word should
End a line and how the syntax
Should turn against the flow
Of lines, which is the skill
That shapes free verse and gives
It organic form. After that came
The more visual patterning of

From *Poems of 1909*

Innocence can never perish;
Blooms as fair in looks that cherish
Dim remembrance of the days
When life was young, as in the gaze
Of youth himself all rose-yclad,
Whom but to see is to be glad.

The Revelation

I awoke happy, the house
Was strange, voices
Were across a gap
Through which a girl
Came and paused,
Reaching out to me—

Then I remembered
What I had dreamed—
A girl
One whom I knew well
Leaned on the door of my car
And stroked my hand—

I shall pass her on the street
We shall say trivial things
To each other
But I shall never cease
To search her eyes
For that quiet look—

The text in *Paterson*, lines
Irregularly spaced and floating
On the field of the page. Then
The next innovation, I think in
About 1953, was the "triadic
Line," which was a step-down
Line of medium length divided
Into three roughly equal parts,
Beginning at the left margin
And cascading gently down to
The right over a series of
Evenly spaced indentations. It
Is the stanzaic base for
"Asphodel, That Greeny Flower,"
Bill's 30-page tribute and
Apology to Floss. Like this:

Of asphodel, that greeny flower,
   like a buttercup
      upon its branching stem—

save that it's green and wooden—
   I come, my sweet
      to sing to you.

We lived long together
   a life filled,
      if you will,

with flowers . . .

The "triadic line" appealed to
Bill for two reasons. It gave
Him more opportunities to use
His gift for beautiful line

Breaks. Second was a practical
Advantage: when he was obliged
To give up his work at the
Hospital because of the strokes
The other doctors made him a
Present of a modern typewriter
That had many improved features.
One of them was a carriage-back
Stop system; he could set the
Stops for the three indents of
The "triadic line" and save the
Bother of trying to get the
Alignment with his shaky hand.

So we come to the final hoped-
For invention of the "variable
Foot," a term first used by Poe.
"Bill was convinced," writes
Herbert Leibowitz, "that our
Poetry needed to find a new
Measure for contemporary
Realities." Bill dreamed that
If he could find the key to
This new measure and master it,
It could become his metrical
Signature. More than that,
And here I'm theorizing, he
Didn't tell me so directly,
It would give him the authority
Of using a disciplined line,
One that could be scanned,
Yet would be free for variety,
For substitutions in the feet.
"He didn't want a rigid foot,"
Leibowitz goes on, "he wanted

A stable foot." The "variable
Foot" would be confirmation that
His poetry could take its place
In the stream of the English
Verse tradition, especially
The great Renaissance poetry
Such as Campion's beautiful:

Harke, al you ladies that do sleep:
    the fayry queen Proserpina
Bids you awake and pitie them that weep:
    you may doe in the darke
What the day doth forbid:
    feare not the dogs that barke,
        Night will have all hid.

Of course Bill was not urging
Rhyme, it was the breaks in the
Scansion that interested him,
And probably also the fact that
Campion too was a doctor.
American speech rhythms were to
Be regularized in some way.
It was a formidable task, but
Much on Bill's mind, as some
Letters to his friends, the
Poet Richard Eberhart and the
Professor John Thirlwall, show:

WCW to Eberhart—10/23/53:

"What Pound did not realize, nor Yeats either, is that a new
order had dawned in the make-up of the poem. The measure,
the actual measure, of the lines is no longer what Yeats was
familiar with. Or Pound either, except instinctively. . . .

196

"Whitman with his so-called free verse was wrong: there can be no absolute freedom in verse. You must have a measure but a relatively expanded measure to exclude what has to be excluded and to include what has to be included. It is a technical point but a point of vast importance."

WCW to Eberhart—5/23/54:

"I have never been one to write by rule, even by my own rules. Let's begin with the rule of counted syllables, in which all poems have been written hitherto. That has become tiresome to my ear.

"Finally, the stated syllables, as in the best of present-day free verse, have become entirely divorced from the beat, that is the measure. The musical pace proceeds without them.
. . .

"By measure I mean musical pace. Now, with music in our ears the words need only be taught to keep as distinguished an order, as chosen a character, as regular, according to the music, as in the best of prose.

"By its *music* shall the best of modern verse be known and the *resources* of the music. The refinement of the poem, its subtlety, is not to be known by the elevation of the words but—the words don't so much matter—by the resources of the music."

That sentence about sound
Mattering more than sense
Would be astonishing given
The nature of his work if we
Were meant to take it literally.
I suspect Bill was only
Inveighing against excessive
Rhetoric and decoration.

197

WCW to Thirlwall—1/13/55:

"If the measure by which the poem is to be recognized has at present been lost, it is only lost in the confusion which at present surrounds our lives. We don't, any more, know how to measure the lines and therefore have convinced ourselves that they can't be measured.

. . .

". . . You cannot break through old customs, in verse or social organization, without drastically changing the whole concept and also the structure of our lives all along the line.

"This is merely and magnificently the birth of a new measure supplanting the old—something we hardly hope to dare."

> In the eight years between this
> Letter and Bill's death in 1963
> One can find a good many more
> References to the "variable foot,"
> Including the lines in "Asphodel,
> That Greeny Flower":
>
> ". . . and set dancing
>   to a measure,
>
> a new measure!
>   Soon lost.
>   The measure itself
>
> has been lost
>   and we suffer for it.
>   We come to our deaths
>
> in silence."

But where is the passage I've
Always hoped to find, no scholar
Has ever pointed me to it, where
Bill demonstrates that he has
Found his grail, the passage
Where he declares without any
Equivocation: "this is my
Variable foot," then defines
Its properties precisely and
Puts the scansion marks to it.

Is there a clue in a poem in
His last book, *Pictures from
Brueghel*, a poem in nine parts,
Which is provocatively titled
"Some Simple Measures in the
American Idiom and the Variable
Foot"? Here, at right, are the
First and last parts. What
Beat do you hear in them?
Can these lines be scanned in
Any formal way? Or can one find
Any significant variations from
What Bill was writing in 1921,
Say at the time of *Sour Grapes*.
The lines are short, the diction
Is skeletal, the typographical
And syllabic patterns are quite
Regular and in large part visual.
I'm afraid for me the poems
Don't show any new measure or
A different rhythm. Am I wrong?

Why didn't Bill find the
"Variable foot" when he was

I. Exercise in Timing

Oh
the sumac died
it's
the first time
I
noticed it

IX. The Stolen Peonies

What I got out of
women
was difficult
to assess Flossie

not you
you lived with me
many years you remem-
ber

that year
we had the magnificent
stand of peonies

how happy we were
with them
but one night

they were stolen
we shared the
loss together thinking

of nothing else for
a whole day
nothing could have

brought us closer
we had been
married ten years

So eager to have it? Was it
Just a mirage? Or was it
Because other poets and
Critics never took his search
Seriously and supported him in
It? Could one incident have
Broken his spirit? Paul
Mariani in his biography tells
Of an evening that might have
Strengthened his morale but
Turned out to be a disaster.
One of Bill's most active
Supporters in the academic
World was Professor Mary
Ellen Solt of the University
Of Indiana. She had written
Frequently on the use of the
"American Idiom" in his work
And on his metrical practices.
Eager to help him along with
The "variable foot," she put
On an evening for Bill and
Floss in Bloomington with
Personal invitations to the
Leading members of the English
Department. Not one of the
Professors came, only students.
This snub by his peers hurt
Bill deeply. And even in his
Talks with students he wasn't
Able to get across what he
Meant by his "variable foot."
He went back to Rutherford in
A state of extreme dejection.

Bill's last year was an
Oppressive sadness for me,
Though his courage was an
Inspiration, his refusal to
Give up on his writing, his
Determination to learn how to
Type again, his handwriting
Being so shaky that even Floss
Could hardly decipher it. What
Could I do to help or comfort
Him? He didn't want a nurse
Hanging around the house. I
Tried to stop by 9 Ridge Road
Now and then. For a few minutes
He would listen to my gossip
About writers, and even smile,
But then he would tire and
Send me away. I felt pretty
Certain from watching him
That ideas for poems were
Forming in his mind even if
He couldn't put them down. Did
I detect occasionally some of
The old snap in his eyes?
I no longer recall the exact
Dates of his strokes, but I
Saw gradual deterioration
Of the whole physical plant.
His eyes were weaker, he took
Longer to summon the words he
Wanted, his reactions were
Slower. Floss said he was
Losing his appetite, some
Evenings all he would eat was

Porridge or a poached egg. He
Was allowed a shotglass of
Bourbon after his dinner but
It didn't perk him up for
Long. He worried about when
Pictures from Brueghel, the
Last book of poems, would be
Ready. Why were the printers
So slow? I took to bringing
The galleys out to him in
Installments as they were
Ready. I read them to him
Line by line, very slowly,
Rereading when he signaled
Me to pause. When he wanted
A correction I'd sit beside
Him on the sofa and painfully
We'd work it out together.
His sense for words, of which
Words would sound well together,
Was as sharp as ever. But he
Became tired so quickly.

One day when I arrived at
9 Ridge Road in the late
Morning I saw an unexpected
And encouraging sight. Bill
Had had a burst of energy and
Was typing, with one finger,
At the dining room table. Floss
Put her head in from the kitchen
To tell me, "Don't disturb him,
He's practicing by trying to
Write me a letter." The floor

Was littered with balls of
Paper Bill had crumpled up
And thrown away. When he was
Tired and stopped his work I
Picked up one of the balls
And deciphered it later
Out in the car. The typing
Was mostly wrong, but this
Is what he wanted to say.

Dear Floss thank you for everything
forgive me   I always loved you   Bill

Miraculously, as Bill kept up
His practice on the machine
He made much improvement so
That his letters were easier to
Understand and Floss could mail
Them. Here is the last letter
To me that he typed himself.

Dear Jim

I fnally got your letter enclosing your letter enclocussing
your letter which was so ompportant foe me, thannkuok
youn very much. In time this fainful bsiness will will soon-
feul will soon be onert. Tnany anany goodness. IfSlossieeeii
wyyonor wy sinfsignature.
I hope I hope I make it   Bill

Bill's battle, the physical battle,
Was ended on March 4, 1963. He had
Died in his sleep in the night;
Floss found him peacefully silent

When she went to wake him for
Breakfast. Not long after, *Pictures
From Brueghel* was awarded the prize
He had never had when he was alive,
The Pulitzer. From then on there
Was steady growth in the popular
Acceptance of Bill's work and its
Recognition in academic circles,
Where it is widely taught in the
Curriculum. He is in all the big
Anthologies. His books have been
Translated into many languages.
The poet who had to pay to get
His first five books published
Is now enshrined as one of the
Great American literary figures.

Bill's funeral was unusual because
The young minister, almost with
Rage, excoriated the prosperous
Elements of Rutherford for never
Realizing that they had a
Genius among them; few of the
"Best people" of the town had
Used "the poet" for their doctor.
As we know from his short stories
His practice was among the poor
And the working people, some of
Whom could only pay him with a
Sack of vegetables from their
Gardens. But Bill had had his
Say about funerals in his poem
"Tract," written back in 1916:

Tract

I will teach you my townspeople
how to perform a funeral
for you have it over a troop
of artists—
unless one should scour the world—
you have the ground sense necessary.

See! the hearse leads.
I begin with a design for a hearse.
For Christ's sake not black—
nor white either—and not polished!
Let it be weathered—like a farm wagon—
with gilt wheels (this could be
applied fresh at small expense)
or no wheels at all:
a rough dray to drag over the ground.
Knock the glass out!
My God—glass, my townspeople!
For what purpose? Is it for the dead
to look out or for us to see
how well he is housed or to see
the flowers or the lack of them—
or what?
To keep the rain and snow from him?
He will have a heavier rain soon:
pebbles and dirt and what not.
Let there be no glass—
and no upholstery, phew!
and no little brass rollers
and small easy wheels on the bottom—
my townspeople what are you thinking of?

A rough plain hearse then
with gilt wheels and no top at all.
On this the coffin lies
by its own weight.

No wreaths please—
especially no hot house flowers.
Some common memento is better,
something he prized and is known by:
his old clothes—a few books perhaps—
God knows what! You realize
how we are about these things
my townspeople—
something will be found—anything
even flowers if he had come to that.
So much for the hearse.

For heaven's sake though see to the driver!
Take off the silk hat! In fact
that's no place at all for him—
up there unceremoniously
dragging our friend out to his own dignity!
Bring him down—bring him down!
Low and inconspicuous! I'd not have him ride
on the wagon at all—damn him—
the undertaker's understrapper!
Let him hold the reins
and walk at the side
and inconspicuously too!

Then briefly as to yourselves:
Walk behind—as they do in France,
seventh class, or if you ride
Hell take curtains! Go with some show

of inconvenience; sit openly—
to the weather as to grief.
Or do you think you can shut grief in?
What—from us? We who have perhaps
nothing to lose? Share with us
share with us—it will be money
in your pockets.
                    Go now
I think you are ready.

                    ◆

At the burial, which took
Place on a slope in the old
Rutherford Cemetery, occurred
An event which to most of those
Present was comical, like the
Clowns piling out of a car at
The circus, but to me, who knew
How to interpret it, was truly
Prophetic. After the service
A huge, unidentifiable, very
Ancient black sedan drew up
On the adjacent roadway, and
From it emerged not one, not
Five, but *ten* blackclad figures,
Dressed in what they thought
Suitable for a funeral, rented
Or borrowed, to join the other
Mourners. They were the leading
Young poets of New York come
To pay homage to the great old
Poet they so much admired. It
Was a striking moment. And it

Was, I knew, symbolic of the
Hundreds and thousands of young
Poets who in the future would
Honor Williams and acknowledge
His influence in their work,
And I one among them.

Now I have talked enough in
Telling what I had to tell.
As an afterpiece I will add
A poem by Kenneth Rexroth
Called "A Letter to William
Carlos Williams," which speaks
For us all and is one of the
Most expressive poems ever
Written by one poet about
Another. Here I will only say
That after all the talk about
His particular achievements
In language, form, and topical
Attitudes Bill remains a person
As complex and indefinable as
Any, yet in his work (as he
Was in his life) believable,
Lovable, and knowable; a great
Poet among all the other great
Poets from first to last to
Whom we turn for consolation,
Friendship, pleasure, wisdom,
And warmth of human feeling.

A Letter to William Carlos Williams

Dear Bill,

When I search the past for you,
Sometimes I think you are like
St. Francis, whose flesh went out
Like a happy cloud from him,
And merged with every lover—
Donkeys, flowers, lepers, suns—
But I think you are more like
Brother Juniper, who suffered
All indignities and glories
Laughing like a gentle fool.
You're in the *Fioretti*
Somewhere, for you're a fool, Bill,
Like the Fool in Yeats, the term
Of all wisdom and beauty.
It's you, stands over against
Helen in all her wisdom,
Solomon in all his glory.

Remember years ago, when
I told you you were the first
Great Franciscan poet since
The Middle Ages? I disturbed
The even tenor of dinner.
Your wife thought I was crazy.
It's true, though. And you're 'pure,' too,
A real classic, though not loud
About it—a whole lot like
The girls of the Anthology.
Not like strident Sappho, who
For all her grandeur, must have

Had endometriosis,
But like Anyte, who says
Just enough, softly, for all
The thousands of years to remember.

It's a wonderful quiet
You have, a way of keeping
Still about the world, and its
Dirty rivers, and garbage cans,
Red wheelbarrows glazed with rain,
Cold plums stolen from the icebox,
And Queen Anne's lace, and day's eyes,
And leaf buds bursting over
Muddy roads, and splotched bellies
With babies in them, and Cortes
And Malinche on the bloody
Causeway, the death of the flower world.

Nowadays, when the press reels
With chatterboxes, you keep still,
Each year a sheaf of stillness,
Poems that have nothing to say,
Like the stillness of George Fox,
Sitting still under the cloud
Of all the world's temptation,
By the fire, in the kitchen,
In the Vale of Beavor. And
The archetype, the silence
Of Christ, when he paused a long
Time and then said, 'Thou sayest it.'

Now in a recent poem you say,
'I who am about to die.'
Maybe this is just a tag

From the classics, but it sends
A shudder over me. Where
Do you get that stuff, Williams?
Look at here. The day will come
When a young woman will walk
By the lucid Williams River,
Where it flows through an idyllic
News from Nowhere sort of landscape,
And she will say to her children,
'Isn't it beautiful? It
Is named after a man who
Walked here once when it was called
The Passaic, and was filthy
With the poisonous excrements
Of sick men and factories.
He was a great man. He knew
It was beautiful then, although
Nobody else did, back there
In the Dark Ages. And the
Beautiful river he saw
Still flows in his veins, as it
Does in ours, and flows in our eyes,
And flows in time, and makes us
Part of it, and part of him.
That, children, is what is called
A sacramental relationship.
And that is what a poet
Is, children, one who creates
Sacramental relationships
That last always.'
    With love and admiration,
    Kenneth Rexroth.

213

THE OLD BEAR:
KENNETH REXROTH

Sometimes he could be sweet as
Honey, but other times he was
Unbearably cranky; you couldn't
Get near him or he'd growl or
Even bite. People either loved
Him or thought he was bad news
And to be avoided at all costs.
That summer when I drove down
From Alta to visit him in San
Francisco he was on a roll of
Good humor and I found him
Quite irresistible. Many of
His stories were made up,
Obvious fictions of a wild
Imagination, but so funny
One wanted to believe them.
When it was time for New
Directions to publish his
Autobiography the lawyer for
The libel-insurance company
Read the script and was
Horrified. "You and this man
Will spend the rest of your
Lives in court." We solved
That problem by changing
Names of the characters who
Would be easy to identify
And making the title *An
Autobiographical Novel.*

When I first saw how thick
Kenneth's manuscript was I
Was surprised. When I dipped
Into it here and there I
Was amazed. I encountered some
Anecdotes that were in Kenneth's
Spicy lingo but could not have
Happened to him, since they
Dealt with people I knew he
Hadn't met—though when he
Was talking he seemed to know
Everyone of any consequence.
It got a bit tiresome this
Omniscience of persons and
I decided to set a little trap
For him. The scene was one
Of Kenneth's "Thursday Nights"
At the old house on Potrero
Hill in San Francisco which
Attracted many of the young
Writers and bohemians from
North Beach. These events
Were Dutch, you had to
Bring your own food and
Drink. For my stunt I
Needed a glib accomplice
And enlisted the poet Robert
Duncan, who was one of the
Favorites of the group. He
Brought the discussion around
To the contemporary French
Poets: Bonnefoy, Guillevic,
Pinget, and others. I chimed
In with a nonexistent poet

Whom I had invented for the
Evening, one Auguste Dampière.
Between us Robert and I gave
Dampière a big build-up; we
Claimed that he was the new
Max Jacob. Kenneth took the
Bait and was soon giving us
The inside dope on his old friend
Auguste. It turned out that he
Had met him in Aix-en-Provence,
Where they had picked up two
Girls at a café and hired a cab
To take them out to visit Mont
Sainte-Victoire, Cezanne's Mont
Sainte-Victoire that is, the hill
That the master had immortalized
More than thirty times in oils
And watercolor. By this time
Kenneth had attained full voice
And there was no stopping him.
After a brief digression on the
Proficiencies of the two young
Ladies from Aix, he gave us
At great length, speaking as
A painter himself, a rundown
On the techniques and spatial
Constructs not only of Cezanne
But of most of the other great
Impressionists, together with
Insights into their private
Lives. It was a masterful
Performance which left Duncan
And me so moved neither of us
Could bring himself to break

The spell by denouncing his
Confabulation, if that is the
Right term for his fakeries.
...

Was another inspiration. They
Were deep in modernism. In 1935
The New Deal's WPA programs for
Artists and writers appealed to
Them as relief for the jobless
But even more politically. They
Were radicals: not communists
But anarchists. Kenneth's
Grandfather had been a friend
Of Eugene Debs, who went to
Jail for building up unions.
Kenneth had been raised on
Proudhon and Bakunin. Andrée
Was a feminist, one of her
Idols was Rosa Luxemburg, the
German revolutionary. Working
Together they did a 100-foot
Mural for a San Francisco
Health center, and Kenneth
Helped edit the California
Guidebook that the WPA
Sponsored. He was an ecologist
Ahead of his time.

TOM MERTON

When I first went down
To Kentucky to meet Merton
At Gethsemani, his monastery
Near Bardstown, the abbot
Had invited me for a visit
After I'd published *Thirty Poems*,
I was expecting gloom and obsession,
Grouchy old monks ponderous
In penitence, glaring through
Their sanctity . . . how wrong I was!
To be sure, the background
Was not prepossessing: a drab
Countryside, scrubby trees,
Dry fields, not verdant,
Shacks and billboards along the
Highway; the buildings
Of the compound behind
Its walls monstrously ugly,
Gray stone blocks set square
Without any architectural
Distinction, the spire
Of the church a tin spike
Poking up at the sky,
Over the gateway, in forbidding
Black letters PAX INTRANTIBUS,
It could have been a prison . . .
How wrong I had been about the inhabitants!
These brothers and monks
Were warriors of joy.
Happy and friendly, laughing

And joking, rejoicing in the
Hard life of work and prayer,
Seven services a day from Vigils
In the dark at 3:15 A.M. through
Lauds, Terce, Sext, None,
Vespers and Compline in the dusk,
These chantings of supplication
For the whole world, even infidels
Not just for the monks.
Such brightness, *lux in aeternitate,*

And Tom (his name now Brother Louis,
As a snake might shed his worldly skin)
The brightest among them, the merriest
Of them all, gaiety exuding
From him. One of the youngest
But already the intellectual
Pivot of the community with
His learning and his comprehension
Of what meditation is all about.
Tom never tried to convert me;
He said if I got grace
It would come from God
Not from his instruction.
He would answer my questions
About theology and the rituals
Very carefully, but no more.
One day we walked up
To the fire tower on the ridge.
Tom was the warden in fire season.
He was good at copping
The best jobs for himself.
He declined to join
The cheese-making crew

Or work in the fields.
And he got out of sleeping
In the dormitory by learning
To snore very loudly,
They gave him an abandoned
Bishop's room all to himself.
We sat in the shelter atop
The fire tower and chewed the fat
About the literary scene, what
The writers were doing. No papers
Or magazines came to the monastery,
The abbot only told the community
In chapter what was suitable
For them to hear. We arranged
How the books of the likes
Of Henry Miller and Djuna Barnes
Would be mailed to the order's
Psychiatrist, who would carry them
To Tom. On the morrow,
By dispensation of the abbot,
Who knew that publishers could
Produce book royalties to the
Benefit of the abbey, Tom
Had leave for the day to be off
With me in my rented car.

When we went out the gate
Past Brother Gatekeeper
Tom was formally dressed
In an old bishop's suit
With celluloid backwards collar.
But when he had finished reading
The day's lesson in his breviary,
And we came to a wood, he said,

Stop here. He hopped out,
Carrying a paper bag. I thought
He was going to pee, but no,
He returned in blue jeans
And an old sweater. Near Salem,
He said, I've heard there's
A good bar. We found it and
Inside, although it was only 10,
A goodly company of jolly farmers.
They looked askance at me
In my city slicker clothes,
But Tom, talking farmer and
Even randy, was an old pal
In fifteen minutes. I didn't drink
Since I was driving, but Tom
Was belting down his first beers
Since he became a novice:
One, two, three . . . at four
I reminded him of our lunch date
In Lexington. Just one more, but
It was two more before I got him out.
Strangely, there was no sign
Of inebriation; he could have been
Drinking Coca-Colas. Our lunch hosts
In their little colonial
House-studio in Lexington
Were the Hammers, gentle
Victor, in his eighties,
In his youth a painter in
Vienna, doing elegant portraits
In the style of Cranach,
And later becoming in America
One of the great hand printers,
His *Hagia Sophia* of Merton's

Being perhaps his masterpiece;
And Carolyn, his wife, younger
Than he, a librarian at the
University who, under his tutelage,
Had become also a renowned printer.

We ate in the garden, talking
About everything except modern art,
Which had to be avoided because
Of Victor's blood pressure.
There was a fine Pommard and after
Coffee Courvoisier, mostly consumed
By Tom but again no sign of his being
Tipsy. Our next stop, heading west,
Was Shakertown. No Shakers left
To do their ecstatic shaking,
But the old buildings and furniture
Well preserved. I started on the
Direct road home but Tom stopped me.
That ham, he said, I remember that
Wonderful ham laced with bourbon
I once had at the inn in Bardstown!
I turned the car and headed for
Bardstown. And it was indeed
A great Kentucky ham, a red-eye ham,
I think they called it, with a bottle of
St.-Émilion to wash it down
And a few nips of cognac
To settle the stomach. And
Tom still sober as a judge.

When we got back to Gethsemani
There wasn't a light in the place.
Brother Gatekeeper was long gone

To his cot in the dormitory.
What to do? I remember, said Tom,
A place on the other side near
The cemetery where the wall
Isn't quite as high as it is here.
Tom was right, the wall was lower.
I got down on all fours
And had Tom stand on my back.
Can you reach the top? I asked.
Just with my fingertips, he said.
OK, hold on if you can,
I'll get up and push up your legs.
Torn was up, lying on the wall but
I couldn't reach his dangling hand.
I thought of my belt. I took it off
And tossed one end up to him.
Brace your legs around the wall
And I'll climb with my legs
The way Rexroth taught me on
Rock faces in the mountains.
Believe it or not, it worked.
We lay in the grass on the far side
Of the wall and laughed and laughed
And laughed. We have done the Devil's
Work today, Tom, I told him.
No, he said, we've been working for
The angels; they are friends of mine.
Keeping very quiet, Tom went off to
His bishop's room, I to my bed
In the wing for the retreatants.

THE RUBBLE RAILROAD

It was October of 1945, only five
Months after the end of World War
Two. I was living in Paris, back
In my old digs in the rue des
Saints-Pères, trying to write a
Novel about life in Pittsburgh
In my youth, but the more I put
Down the worse it got. So I was
Glad when I had a letter from my
Old friend Herbert Blechsteiner
In Cologne saying that he had
Been able to wangle the use of
An Army car, with driver and
Gas ration, and would I like to
Join him for a week to inspect
What was left of Germany after
The bombing. Herbert, who was
Fluent in six languages, was
The greatest wangler I ever
Encountered. Anything he wanted
He would get, and at a bargain
Price. And he would do the
Same for his friends. This
Genius came from his years in
The Middle East. He had been
Born into a large family who
Were traders in antiquities.
There were branches of Blech-
Steiner Ltd. from Bombay to
Lisbon, all run by Herbert's

Uncles or cousins. London was
The province of Herbert's
Brother Ulrich, with a rather
Grand shop on Jermyn Street
Not far from the Cavendish
Hotel, where Rosa Lewis, one
Of the mistresses of Edward VII,
Still held sway. Herbert had
Served an apprenticeship at the
Shop in Damascus, where he
Picked up spoken Arabic, but
His heart was in languages and
Writing. He came back to Paris,
Where he lived with the uncle
There and did his time at the
Sorbonne in linguistics.

I took the Berlin Express but
Got off at Mannheim to board a
Steamer down the Rhine, this for
The sight of the Rhenish castles
Perched on the hilltops and
Vineyards cascading down to the
River. In Cologne I found a
Daimler-Benz sedan parked at
The Hotel Gruber. It had a
Little U.S. Army pennant on the
Front mudguard, so that would
Be Herbert. The driver, a sergeant,
Seeing my bag, leapt from the
Car to open the door and salute.
This saluting bit went on all
Through the trip. It embarrassed
Me because I'd managed with
Some effort to avoid the war.

"Can't you get him to stop the
Saluting?" I asked Herbert,
Who replied, "I told him you were
A bigshot in the OSS." I'd been
Wondering for some time why
Herbert stayed on with the army
As only an interpreter. That
Evening at Die Drei Hirsche
(Herbert would know the best
Place to eat in any city) over
A fine bottle of Gewürztraminer,
He explained that Germany was
Awash with displaced artworks.
Some were things that GI's had
Stolen. Others were things that
Starving owners who didn't have
Enough food cards for their
Families had to sell, often for
A song. Herbert's business was
To pick up such treasures and
Get them out to his relatives
In the Blechsteiner offices in
Army mail pouches which weren't
Censored. And how, I asked, did
He come by such an elegant auto?
Kindness of a brigadier, he told me,
A charming fellow from New York
Who was a collector of etchings.
"I got him a prime Dürer, museum
Quality. He couldn't do enough
For me."

Next morning I accompanied Herbert
On his rounds. He needed some cash
And tackled a fat little dealer

Whose luxurious shop near the Dom
Betokened a sharpie set to catch
Tourists. Herbert was showing him
A superb Tibetan devil tanka he
Had picked up from one of the
Gurkhas in a British regiment that
Was stationed near Hanover. The
Dealer was no match for Herbert's
Salesmanship, which included verse
Quotations supposedly from the
Book of the Dead. Spotting me as
An American, Herr Plumps brought
Out a painting which he claimed
Was a Franz Marc, one of the
Blaue Reiter group, the man who
Did the famous bright red horses.
It was handsome, but Herbert
Pulled his ear to signal me that
It was a fake. And we left the shop.

Setting out for Frankfurt we
Stopped at the railroad station
To pick up the magnificent
Alexander who arrived from
Berlin to join up with us. I
Have selected the adjective
With care. Alexander Gruener,
Who had been Herbert's night
And day companion throughout
The war, was the embodiment
Of Hitler's prescription for
The ideal Teuton: nearly two
Meters tall, shoulders like
An ox but waist like a wasp;

Blue eyes, blond hair, and
A mien serious with determination;
His only shortcoming was that he
Was at heart a communist, which
Made him acceptable to Herbert as
A lover. The first few days we
Were together Alexander viewed
Me with suspicion, he couldn't
Quite place me in relation to
Herbert. Was I a rival? But he
Gradually got the picture that
We were just friends. He relaxed
And we got on well. His idea of
Amusements was to correct my
German and make the conventional
European's jokes about America.
He was soon calling me "der
Cowboy" and demonstrating his
Prowess in arm wrestling.

The bombing damage that we had
Seen in Cologne was slight; it
Had not been a primary target.
But Frankfurt was another story.
The center of the city had been
Flattened. Beautiful old quarters
Which I remembered from earlier
Visits were a desolation of
Destruction. The madness of war.
While we were in Germany I kept
A diary. When I got back to
Paris I put parts of it into verse:

In Frankfurt

Gray hungry men are loading
debris from a blasted house
into the little dump cars of
the rubble railroad
     this is
the line that makes its run
from death to hope
       its tracks
are laid on blocks in every
German city & when one street
is cleaned they move them to
the next
    it pays no dividends
but runs all day and will for
7 years
    their shovels probing
hunger-slowly in the settled
wrack turn up a twisted, rust-
ing spoon. They all put down
their tools and pass it around
appraising worth or use
        but
it's too bad they toss it in
the cart
    I pick it out and put
it in my pocket
      I want that
spoon
   they stare I blush and
offer cigarettes they take &
thank and I walk off
      I want

their spoon I'll take it home
back to the other world. I'll
need it there to learn to eat.
The men, and there were women
too in the work crews, were a
miserable looking group. They
were obviously undernourished,
dressed in rags, some of the
men in remnants of Wehrmacht
uniforms, all of them so tired
they had to rest, leaning on
their shovels every few minutes.

How Did They Look?

The face narrows
the skin tightens on the cheekbones
the mouth & lips tighten
the cheeks suck in a bit
the eyes sink back into the skull
the eyes are dull seeming
the circles under the eyes deepen
and darken
the hair thins and grays
that's just the head
the body?
I couldn't bear to look.

Heading to Munich we couldn't
Go by the autobahn because it
Had only been rebuilt in sections.
Better to head south on small
Roads where we could enjoy the
Countryside, zigzagging from one

Rural road to another. It was
A welcome escape from the wreckage
Of the war. Pristine villages
Where the farming life was still
Going on. Hedgerows and poplar
Trees separating the meadows.
But there were few cows or sheep
In the meadows. They had been
Eaten. Where we stopped for
A lunch of *Kaiserschmarren* in
An inn there was a small
Church beside the place, one
That had the Slavic onion
Top on its spire. There a peasant
Wedding was taking place which
We watched for a half-hour.
No cars about, there was so
Little gas. The bride and groom
Went off in a farm cart drawn
By a white horse so ancient he
Could hardly walk. We made a
Dip down to the Danube to see
The great Gothic cathedral at
Ulm which had not been hurt.

In Munich we linked up with
An old friend of Herbert's,
The famous photographer Max
Faber. Max was touring around
Germany shooting the ruins for
The air force, which wanted a
Record of their handiwork for
The Allied archives. He showed
Us his portfolio. Many of his
Shots were magnificent as art,

Giant sculptures in their way,
Especially where they dealt
With tall buildings that had
Only partially collapsed. The
Work depressed Max. In
His ebullient, gay way he was
A very jolly fellow, full of
German and macabre Jewish jokes
And stories. We spent a lot of
Time going around Munich with
Him. The sights of destroyed
Munich hurt me more than had
Frankfurt because I knew the
City well from the summer when
I had lived there, quartered with a
German family who were supposed
To teach me some German. I was
Only seventeen then, much more
Interested in the *Mädels* I
Picked up at the opera and in
The big English Garden Park.
Although the factories which
Were the targets for the air
Raids were outside the city
Proper, the aim of those who
Released the bombs was not
Good. Many of the cultural
Monuments were demolished.
Both of the Pinakotheks had
Been hit, though fortunately
The paintings had been hidden
In salt mines and mountain
Caves. The buildings on both
Sides of the regal avenues,
The Maximilienstrasse and the

Ludwigstrasse, were smashed.
The Wittelsbach palaces were
Down, and in the business center
The Marienplatz and the rathaus
Town hall were in bad shape.

As we wandered about the city,
Where rubble railroads and
Their crews were working here
And there, we noticed another
Presence: large numbers of
American soldiers. They didn't
Seem to be doing anything except
Killing time. I talked to
A few of them to get a
Feel of how, as they waited
To be shipped home, they
Felt about their situation
As conquerors of an old
Culture. And about the
Desolation their planes
Had wrought. Their chief
Expressions were of boredom
And of anger that repatriation
Was taking so long. I tried
Later to get it down in a poem.

Song of the GI's and the MG's

We are the lords of the cigarette
    & the green passport
        we do the best we can
we rule the world unwillingly
    & have good intentions
        we do the best we can

234

we are most of us sorry that you
   are always so hungry
      we do the best we can
we are unaccustomed to governing
   & make some mistakes
      we do the best we can
we often marry your girls after we
   have seduced them
      we do the best we can
we are hurt when you resist our plans
   for your re-education
      we do the best we can
we will help you try to clean up
   the bomb mess we made
      we do the best we can
we are the lords of the cigarette
   & the green passport
      we really do mean to do
      the best we can for you.

One evening Max invited us out to
His place in Schwabing, the artists'
Quarter out Ludwigstrasse beyond
The Siegestor. That is the quarter
Renowned for Oktoberfests, a week
Of merriment and carousing as famed
As our Mardi Gras in New Orleans.
There wouldn't be one that year,
Of course, but I hear now that it's
Going strong as ever again. Max's
Residence could hardly be called
An apartment. One side wall of
The building had been bombed off,
But Max had made a false wall
With canvas nailed onto salvaged

Posts. Electric power had not yet
Been restored but there were half a
Dozen candles. Max had an army friend
And there was Jack Daniels from the
PX. He had assembled some artists
And several pretty girls. It was
An eventful party as this poem
Tells it, not a happy one for the girl.

Max's Party

One of our new aristocrats
the knights of the air en-
thralls (he thinks) a half-
starved German tart with his
exploits while he gets drunk
then he passes out poor girl
she has to hit the street again
without a meal the MP's
cart him off in their jeep.

And one of the artists
Had a tale to tell.

Hard to Translate

My friend Klaus a German goes
to the MG travel office for a
permit to visit Switzerland old
            friends in Berne

have invited him they will feed
and fatten him for three weeks and
clear some of the misery mist
            out of his brain

The MG official feels like a little
joke and kids Klaus "why ever
do you want a trip? you Germans
        should stay here

at home and enjoy your hunger-
strafe" (that word is rather hard
to translate as it means hunger-
        punishment but it

also suggests the strafing that
God was supposed to give to the
English) Klaus winces but keeps
        hold of his tem-

per he patiently tells the man
(who is a Jew) about his impris-
onment under the Nazis in the
        end he gets his

permit all right the man is a
good egg and meant to give it
to him all the time he was just
        feeling like his

little joke but he should not
have said that Klaus tells me
such things go to the bone and
        they stick there.

My happiest day in Munich was
When I took the little local train
South to Gauting, a village which is
Halfway to the Starnbergersee,
To visit the Heys, the family

With whom I had spent the summer
Years before to learn German.
Such nice people. I was sad
When I'd heard recently that
They were in terror of the Nazis.
They weren't Jews but the son,
Fritzi, had been expelled from
Munich University. The father
Who painted artwork for post–
Cards was in trouble because
He had declined to paint
The leader of a Nazi parade.

Every Saturday when I left them
I feared I might not see them again.
But when I called on the Heys
Now all seemed well. I walked out
To their house from the Gauting
Station and nothing was changed
Except that the watchdog Günter
Had expired. Herr Hey was painting
Away in his attic studio. He
Had received a commission from
The Prinzregenten Theatre to do
Cards from scenes of Mozart's
Operas. They read me letters
From Fritz who had escaped
To India and was finishing
His engineering degree at the
University of Allahabad. And
There, my special blessing, was
Dear Frau Hey working in her
Beautiful flower garden. She
Was the one who was in charge

Of my German lessons. How I
Vexed her because I had
"Ungenügende Anlegung"
For irregular verbs and things
That required memorization.
But she was gentle in her
Reproaches; she remembered
What it was like to be a
Student at seventeen. She
Imposed no penalties. I
Could take the train in to
Munich for the opera as often
As I wanted as long as I
Was back by midnight.

My best friend was my bicycle.
After lunch I'd take off on
It riding for miles through
The manicured paths of the
Towering forests. Peasants
Picked up every stick and
Carted them home on their
Little handcarts. *"Grüss
Gott,"* I would shout to the
Gatherers as I pedaled
Past them, and *"Grüss Gott
Herr"* they would reply from
The shadowy depths of the
Forest. If it was a warm day
I would ride down to the top
Of the Starnbergersee, a
A big lake that runs nearly to the
Foot of the Alps. There was
A *Schwimmbad* there where I'd

Change into my trunks and
Rent a bathchair in which I
Could stretch out to sun
Myself as I looked up at the
Mountains, the Alps above
Garmisch and Mittenwald
With the top of the mighty
Zugspitze peering over them.
One day I fell asleep in
The sun. When the old man
Who ran the *Schwimmbad* woke
Me up I saw that I was the
Last. "You should have
Wakened me," I told him.
"No," he said, "I looked you
Over and could tell that
You were having a good
Dream. That's what all of us
In this country need now, a few
Good dreams."

Herbert and Alexander wanted
Me to drive up to Berlin with
Them but I'd had enough of
Ruins and suffering people.
I took the train from Munich
To Paris and tried to buckle
Down to work on my novel.
But it was hard to concentrate.
Pittsburgh suddenly seemed like
A place that never existed
In real life. What I had seen
In Germany kept flooding my
Brain. It was a long time, even

After I'd returned to the States,
Before I was able to put my
Heart in the book. One day as
I was avoiding work, this little
Poem appeared on my notebook
Page. It had written itself.

O Frères Humains

The rubble railroad
carries freight
that's more than loads
of stone and dirt
it carries off
an age's hate
and puts it with
a people's heart

the cars are dumped
beyond the city
and then come back
to load once more
o brother men
at last learn pity
return them full
with love to share.

It was in London that I
Fell into the wrong bed.
I should have guessed she
Was paranoid but sometimes
You can't tell. She picked
Me up in the Gargoyle. It
Was the night Dylan tripped
And sprained his ankle so
Badly he couldn't walk.
We got him to his place in a
Taxi, then went on to hers
In Chelsea. I think her
Name was Moira but I can't
Remember for sure now. She
Was a small girl, brown hair,
Lively eyes, nicely dressed,
An upper-class accent, quite
Chatty. She had some bottles
And we drank till we both
Passed out with our clothes
On. Next day, about noon,
She ordered a car with a
Driver and we drove down to
Bath. That's when the bad talk
About Americans started, but
I let it pass. She had friends
In Bath, a couple with an
Apartment in the Crescent.
We dumped on them; they said
We could have the sofa. We

Ate at a pub, then the drink
Began again. I think I was
The first to pass out. I woke
Up in the night. She was on
The sofa with the man. No sign
Of the wife, I went back
To sleep on the floor.

Next morning when the couple
Had gone off, they had a
Shop somewhere, she said,
"Well, you brought me down
Here, I guess I'd better
Let you have it." She sat
Down on the sofa and pulled
Up her skirt. By then I
Wasn't interested, but she
Gibed at me: "Come on, Yank,
Let's see what you're good
For." When that was over,
And it wasn't much, there
Was the only kind word I
Heard about Americans. She
Said, "You're better than
Most of the Johnnies around
Here." I should have left
Her in Bath to get herself
Home, but I felt sorry for
Her somehow. She was a mess
But sort of pitiful. I got
Her back to Chelsea. She
Didn't ask me in. The car
Hires ran me sixty pounds.

THE YELLOW PAD

That's where it all gets piled
Up, on the blue lines of the
Big yellow pads, when I'm wakened
In the middle of the night by the
Pressure of images and words at
The back of my brain, ideas that
Are struggling to escape, to be
Liberated from the labyrinth of
Lost memories. The rush of them
Is strong enough to jolt me out
Of sound sleep.
                              Last night the
Images were of Liddy and the
Words were the way she talked.
(This was forty years ago.)
She had a little resonant
Throatiness in her voice that
Set her apart from other girls
From Brooklyn. Poor Liddy, I
Treated her shamefully as only
A horny young man on the loose
Could do. She wasn't a beauty,
But she had a bright, pert
Look, a teasingness in her
Eyes that commanded attention.
Black hair and a dark com-
Plexion. Her body spoke to me
Like that of one of the girls
You read about in the Old
Testament. It was fecund. She
Moved in a way that made her

Hips glide. She was *attirante*,
As the French might say, she
Was seductive.
                    Liddy was a
Clerk in the magazine office
Where I was then working.
My first job in the city.
It wasn't long before we
Were eying each other, then
Talking more than was neces-
Sary for work, then going
Out for lunch together and
Then after just a few weeks
Making love on the couch
That opened into a day bed
In my little one-room apart-
Ment on 73rd Street. She was
Far from being an innocent
Virgin. She suggested things
To do that I had never done
Before. She was proud of
Her skill and knowledge. It
Was all in a spirit of fun
And games. But there was
One strange thing: she never
Let me touch her breasts.
I could kiss them but was
Not allowed to play with
Them. Little spheres with
Nipples that went hard, but
She would slap my hand away.
But she was good inside,
Like honey. She was ready
For more than I could often
Give. But it came to me

245

Clearly after a month that
She wanted to be serious
About me that she hoped to
Get married. A good Jewish
Girl gets married even if
It's to a goy, as long as
He has a job and is making
Money. It became a conflict
Of wills, my lust against
Her determination. Oh, she
Attacked with great guile.
Nothing was ever openly
Said about marriage, but
She exerted all her sexual
Power. She began to invite
Me to spend a weekend now
And then at her apartment
On Cumberland Street in
Brooklyn. She was a good
Cook and she spoiled me.
Candles and wine on the
Table. Sometimes we would
Go to the opera or to the
Ballet. She read books
That were above her back-
Ground to please me. She
Had a good IQ and talked
Well about what she read.
In the mornings we would
Sleep late, then take our
Showers together, soaping
Each other under the spray
And rubbing our slippery
Bodies against each other.
Then she would do breakfast

But without dressing. She
Would dart about her little
Kitchen without a stitch on,
Pausing now and then to kiss
Me intimately.

But all the while I was
Enjoying her, playing with
Her for my pleasure, I knew
Our relationship could
Never be altered. There
Was the barrier of class,
Of cultural background
Between us. I couldn't
Take her out with my class–
Mates from Harvard and she
Never took me to meet her
Parents. It was unthinkable
That I would have her meet
Mine. She understood only
Too well what worried me,
And she made a last effort
To convince me that what
We shared was enough to
Bind us together. Still
There was no discussion of
The problem. It was all
Intuitive, like a groping
Game of blindman's buff.

She had never been skiing
But she persuaded me to
Take her up to New Hamp–
Shire for a weekend. She
Bought a ski outfit at

Saks so she would look
Right. I put her in the
Ski class for beginners
And she didn't do badly.
The crisis came when we
Were in the Pullman car
That night to go back to
New York. I asked her to
Take the lower berth but
After the train got going
And the other passengers
Had retired she opened
The curtains and pulled me
Into the lower berth with
Her. I couldn't resist the
Exotic temptation. At first
She was gentle but soon
She became violent. Her
Fingers were like talons
Gripping my body. She began
To bite me, then to engorge
Me. She wanted to mouth
Every part of me, to swallow
Me entire. She was possessed.
I was saved by the cries and
Groans of her frenzy. The
Black porter heard them and
Put his head into the opening
Of the curtains, "Everything
All right, suh?" he asked.
I told him it was all right
And he went away. Now Liddy
Went from passion to fright.
She began to shake as if

She were having an epileptic
Fit. I held her in my arms
For hours but the attack
Persisted on and off. When
We reached Grand Central
I found a cab and took her
Out to Brooklyn. Neither
Of us said much and when I
Tried to hold her hand she
Pulled it away. We both knew
That our relationship was
Over. It was the end of
The line for us.

When I got to the office
That morning Liddy was not
There and she didn't come
In all day. That night she
Came when nobody was there
And cleaned out her desk.
She never wrote or called
And I've never seen her
Again.

Poor little Liddy, I still
Think of her now and then.
I reproach myself for any
Selfishness and for not
Having found a way to make
The parting less cruel for
Her. Now and then I'd hear
About her from the girls
She'd known in the office.
They told me that she had

Had to go to a shrink for
Many months to get back her
Peace of mind and her self-
Esteem. Through one of the
Girls I sent her a check
But she never cashed it.
Two years later I learned
That she'd married well, a
Professor of history at
Barnard. I hope Liddy is
Happy now and has forgiven
Me for making her a victim.
I used her shamelessly. It's
All down on my yellow pad.

THE DESERT IN BLOOM

Why can't you remember the Nevada
Desert awash with bright-colored
Flowers when we camped not far
From Tonopah that April long ago?
It was soon after we had met in
San Francisco and fallen in love.
You were George's sister, the
Beautiful poet's beautiful sister.
That's how I got to know you.
Surely you must remember how the
Desert that was so harsh all the
Rest of the year, rocks and gray
Sand, had suddenly burst into
Bloom, a salute to Persephone in
Almost violent praise of spring,
A salute that would last only a
Few weeks till the snow moisture
In the ground would be exhausted.
Rexroth had loaned us a tent and
We gathered dry cactus to cook
Over an open fire. At night we
Heard the soft cooing of doves
From all around us in the dark
But at dawn they ceased their
Complaining. You said that they
Reminded you of the doves in
Provence when you were there
As a girl, the *roucoulement des
Colombes* that the troubadours
And their ladies had heard in

The castle gardens, recording
Their sound in their *cansos*.

The ground was hard under our
Sleeping bags, the desert gets
Chilly at night, so cold that
Sometimes we had to squeeze
Into one bag, skin to skin,
Enlaced together. At night in the
Desert the stars seem twice as
Bright as anywhere else; when
We lay on our backs we would
Look up into the vastness, trying
To locate the constellations
And remember the names that were
Given them by the Greeks in the
Myths how many thousands of years
Ago. Andromeda and the Dioscuri,
Cassiopeia, whom Perseus saved
From the sea monster; Orion, the
Mighty hunter; the Pleiades, whose
Comings and goings tell the seasons;
Berenike, whose pretty lock of
Hair has lived in song; the lion,
The dragon, and the swan. Your
People were Jewish but your
Beauty was more of Attica than
Of Phoenicia, great brown eyes,
Dark hair and olive skin. The
Girls of Lesbos would have adored
You but you were not of their
Kind. Your body is described
In the *Song of Songs*; not a
Fraction of an inch would

Have changed in its proportions
If I were a sculptor. The desert
Was empty and I would ask you
To lie naked in the sun, now
And then changing your pose, a
Moving sculpture. You had the
Marks of Eros, a girl fit for
The Mysteries. Liquid as the
Fountain Arethusa. And you were
Funny and endearing and passionate.
Holding hands, we took walks on
The endless desert before the sun
Became too hot. I picked flowers
And made a multicolored garland
For your hair. The handmaiden
Of Aphrodite, *venerandam*. In the
Shade of the tent I read you the
Exquisite love sonnets of Louise
Labé, which aroused me to make
Love again, hot as it was, the
Sweat glistening on our bodies.

One day we drove into Tonopah,
Now the slumbering ruin of the
Old hell-&-damnation mining
Town, where once fortunes of
Gold were won and lost at the
Tables, and men killed for it.
The streets were empty, but in
What is left of the Grand Hotel
California we found an old man
Dozing on top of the green
Gaming table; we woke him up
And shot craps with silver dollars

For chips. We stayed on the desert
For three days, when we had used
Up the water we had brought in
Cans.

Now after fifty years we're in
Touch again. You've had four
Husbands and I'm on my third
Marriage. You say that you
Can hardly remember our love-
Making on the flowering desert.
How can that be? For me it's
As fresh as if it only happened
Yesterday. I see you clear with
My garland in your hair. Now we
Are two old people nursing our
Aches. What harm can there be
In remembering? We cannot hurt
One another now.

IN TRIVANDRUM

My next stop in India that year
(Which was 1953, as best I can
Recall) was Trivandrum, a little
But lovely city in the region now
Known as Kerala, which was in
Colonial times a princely state
Ruled by the Portuguese, then
The Dutch, and then the English,
Who called it Cochin. Vasco da
Gama landed his ships at
Cochin in 1502, reckoning it the
Finest port on the Arabian Sea
South of Bombay. Cochin has a
Heavy rainfall, making the land
Rich for rice, tapioca, pepper, and
Vegetables. The landscape is set
With graceful coconut palms and
Many ponds and little ornamental
Waterways. The language mainly
Is Malayalam, but Trivandrum
Holds also a settlement of Jews
That boasts the oldest synagogue
In Asia. Christians of differing
Sects are scattered all over the
Subcontinent. Many myths tell
Of the coming of Christianity
To India. In Malabar they think
The Apostle Thomas ("doubting
Thomas") arrived in Cochin in
A.D. 52 to take up the work of
Conversion. But on the eastern

255

Coast people tell you Thomas
Built his church in Madras on
A hill known as The Mount.

I had come to Trivandrum to
Meet the novelist Raja Rao.
Along with R.K. Narayan of
Mysore, Raja Rao was, in those
Days and probably still is, the best
Indian writer working in English.
(How good the native writers
May be, since they compose in
thirteen major languages, is
Hard to guess. Few of them can
Read the works of the others.)
But I had read Raja Rao's novel
The Serpent and the Rope and I
Had no doubt in my mind that
He was first class. I had heard
Rumors that he had finished
A new novel. I wanted to find
Him. The rumors were true.
After we had been together for
Two days, during which Raja
Had assessed my enthusiasm
For Indian life and culture, he
Placed the manuscript of his
New book, *Kanthapura*, in my
Hands, saying: "I think you'll
Like this. My friend Mr. Forster
Has been over it and says it's
A good book about India as
She is today, after Gandhi."
I didn't need Forster's praise to

Convince me that this was a
Masterpiece. *Kanthapura* is
A book like no other I'd read,
A magical book that brings the
Spell of India to the western
Reader. New Directions brought
The book out at once, and after
Many reprintings it remains
As fresh and compelling as it
Was when I first encountered it.

"Kanthapura" is a typical small
Village of southern India in
Which the changing life of all
Castes, impacted by Gandhi's
Revolution of independence
From the British, is the main
Force. Young Moorthy, back
From the city with "new ideas,"
Works to break down the old
Barriers. Nonviolence, as
Gandhi taught it, is his way
Of mobilizing the villagers to
Action. But his efforts are met
With violence from the police
And the rich landowners. The
Remarkable thing in the book
To me is its colloquial manner.
Rao's narrator is an old woman
Of the village who is imbued
With the legendary history of
Her region, the old traditions
Of Hinduism and the Vedic
Myths. She knows the past.

The stories of the villagers,
And her commentary on her
Neighbors is both pungent and
Wise. In her speech are echoes
Of the traditional folk epics
Such as the *Ramayana*. But
How does Rao manage this
When writing in plain lucid
English? He has somehow
Made us hear native speech
In his narrator's extraordinary
Anglo-Indian language. He
Has a fine ear. He had known
The intonations and rhythms
Of the villagers as a child when
He was growing up in Mysore.
Then, because he came from
A prominent family, he had
Opportunities unusual for
An Indian, the University of
Madras and study in France at
Montpellier and the Sorbonne.

Traipsing about the countryside
With Raja as my guide was a
Great pleasure. The land is so
Verdant, and the busy life of
The inland waterways delighted
Me, the small open ferryboats,
Mostly motorized but now and
Then a boat with the red lateen
Sails of the ancient Arab dhows
That had first opened up the
Malabar coast. Raja had no

Car, but we borrowed bicycles
With which we followed the
Footpaths or the rough roads
Created by old bullock carts
Whose once-round wheels
Had been worn squarish by
Long use. We saw the villagers
Ploughing with their cattle,
Humped slaves who would work
Every day until they dropped,
Sleeping nights out in the rain.

Yet these cows seemed to live
A happier life than the sacred
Cows you find in Calcutta who
Live in the streets, sleep on the
Sidewalks, and are fed by the
Faithful—once I was watching
As children gave candy bars
To a Calcutta cow—all this
Because the people believe
That cattle are descended, at
Least symbolically, from those
The Gopis watched over for
Lord Krishna at Brindaban.
We saw sheep and chickens
Around the hutments but no
Pigs. Little monkeys aplenty in
The coconut palms. The men
Distill a palm wine which they
Call "toddy." We were offered
Cups of it which tasted so awful
I could scarcely get mine down
Out of politeness. It looked like

Rotten eggs. But the intoxicating
Effect is said to be considerable.
Knowing Malayalam, Raja Rao
Was able to converse with the
People, who were not shy. They
Gathered around us to talk and
Raja interpreted for me. He said
They had never seen anyone
As tall as I (I'm six-foot five).
They wanted to know where I
Came from and what I ate to
Get so big. Did I practice yoga?
Or some other occult mastery?

Some of them invited us into
Their thatched huts to show
Us with pride the rice-paste
Abstract paintings on their
Walls and thresholds. Raja
Taught me on that visit to
Eat curry and other Indian
Foods with my fingers, for no
Brahmin would ask for utensils.
It would be a breach of the rules
Of caste. But don't ask me to
Show you how it's done; I was
A poor pupil. The weather was
Hot in Cochin, of course, all
That moisture with the sun
Smoldering down through it.
Raja loaned me a dhoti, much
Better than my European pants
And shirt. But I managed more
Than once to get the skirt of

My dhoti caught in my bicycle
Chain, with resultant tumbles.
Our audience was amused. In
The evenings we had our curry
At Raja's home, which was for
Me a further trial of the fingers
In place of a fork. His was an
Extended family living in a
Small house in Trivandrum
And to this day I'm not sure
Who was who. Many women
In their saris smiled at me and
Said nothing. Only the men
Joined us at table. The women
Ate apart, maybe in the kitchen
Which I was not shown. Then
Raja and I went out to wander
The streets of the old town with
Its Dutch-style buildings. Parts
Of it could have been Delft or
Nijmegen. No street lights, not
Much light from the house
Windows; it was eerie. Bare
Feet in the darkness making
No noise. It was enchanting too.

We went to a show by
A troupe of Kathakali dancers
—Very exciting. Most of the
Dancing in South India, such
As the gliding style of Bharata
Natya, is tranquil, except for
An accompaniment of soft
Drumming; movement is

By the arms and hands, and
The "story" is told in classic
Mudras that have assigned
Meanings. Kathakali however
Is the opposite, violent motion
Most of the time. In a way it
Reminded me of the dramatic
Posturing in Japanese Kabuki.
For the westerner one of the
Attractions of Kathakali is
The costumes. Also the masks
Of the male dancers, sculpted
And grotesque. Vivid primary
Colors. Faces to scare children.
Demons and heroes. Men as
Tigers, as serpents. Terrifying.
Much magic, much death.

The plays are given outdoors
And always at night, often not
Finishing until the dawn. In
Darkness the great brass lamps
Flicker and add to the mystery.
The audience sits on the ground
(Though Raja Rao and I were
Honored with chairs). Men,
Women and children usually
Are separated. Two drummers,
Sounding their drums with
Their hands, often in very fast
Rhythms, provide the music.
The actors speak passages of
Verse that narrate the action
Of the play. The dialogue is

Sung by two singers who stand
At the back of the "stage." Now
The stories of the plays are told
In Malayalam rather than the
Classic Sanskrit. but they are
Still the ancient texts, epics like
The *Ramayana* (which reports
The heroic adventures of Rama
When he rescues his wife from
The demon-king Ravana of
Ceylon) or the *Mahabharata*
(Which recounts the endless
Struggle between two families,
The Pandavas and Kauravas,
Though the preeminent hero
Of the poem is the god Krishna).
Or the *Gita Govinda* (a cycle of
Poems about Krishna). These
Are traditional tales known
Almost universally in India
To all classes, just as Greek
Myths and Bible stories
Are known to us in the West.
In origin they go back perhaps
A dozen thousand years to
The oral tradition of village
Storytellers, the entertainers
Of that culture, just as our
Homeric epics are thought
To have been composed and
Revised and embellished by
Generations of warrior poets
Who recited them around the
Smoky campfires of ancient

Armies. At some point these
Original Hindu poems were
Transcribed into Sanskrit by
The pandits and gurus. Then
The final step was translation
Into the various vernaculars,
Hindi, Urdu, Tamil, Marathi,
Malayalam, and many others.
The evening of Kathakali was
Dramatic and thrilling though
Very long: it went on way past
Midnight. Raja Rao briefed me
On the unfolding motifs and
Action as the play progressed.
Then the next day at dusk we
Experienced something even
More remarkable. Through Rao
I had met Professor Vivekananda
Who taught in the college at
Ernakulam on the coast north
Of Trivandrum. Vivekananda
Knew Sri Nalanda, a Vedantist
Guru from Bombay who was
Visiting friends in a small
Village in the Cardamom
Hills. It was a rough trip
Getting there in a jitney
But we made it and the sage
Welcomed us cordially to one
Of the most intense occasions
Of my visit. I wouldn't have
Believed the background story
Vivekananda told me about Sri
Nalanda if we had been in any

Country but India, where the
Occurrence of wonders is so
Continual and many minds
Are saturated with the occult.
Gurus, holy men, sadhus, yogis.
Sannyasis all over the place,
Some with begging bowls, or
Smeared with ashes, or naked
In the streets. Being holy, being
A devotee of this god or that,
Depending on handouts from
The public, is a way of life.

I was told by Vivekananda that
Nalanda came from a favored
Middle-class family. He had
Done well at school and had
Entered the railway service,
Where he had also done well,
Ending up as superintendent
At Bangalore. A faultless
Reputation, a married family
Man; no hint of any instability.
But his whole life was changed
When one night, while taking
A walk in the countryside, he
Met with a celestial messenger.
He knew by the godlike
Aura radiating around the
Old man's head that this
Stranger by the roadside was
Heaven-sent. The ancient
Invited Nalanda to sit on the
Edge of a ditch and said that he

Had flown from Dharmsala
In the Himalayas to instruct
Nalanda, who indeed believed
It because like all Indians he
Believed in parakinesis. He
Knew that servants of the gods,
Like the apsarases, could move
Themselves over thousands of
Miles in the blink of an eye.
They talked together all night.
Then at dawn the messenger
Vanished, but not until he had
Laid on Nalanda the solemn
Injunction to make himself
A serious teacher of Vedanta.
Nalanda was careful to keep
What had happened a secret,
But immediately he began to
Study Vedanta with the wise
Men of the region, giving up
His worldly aspirations, and
He undertook long hours of
Meditation. In a few years he
Was renowned as an adept in
The doctrines of Vedanta and
Their significance, and also as
An eloquent elucidator of the
Ultimate meaning of reality,
Which, as it descends from the
Ancient Vedic texts such as the
Upanishads, concerns especially
The state of being beyond good
And evil, existence beyond and
Above mere knowledge. Then

Sri Nalanda was ready to begin
His teaching, and soon many
Devotees were attracted to him.

On the night of my visit to him
With Professor Vivekananda
The setting for Sri Nalanda's
Lecture was not unlike that of
The Kathakali. It was outdoors
But a tarpaulin extended over
The bath chair in which the sage
Reclined as he talked. He was a
Small man whose somewhat
Birdlike features were belied
By a deep, almost hoarse voice,
More military than priestly.
His head was bald and glinted
As if astrally in the flaring light
Of the brass lanterns. He had
Piercing black eyes. He wore a
White dhoti and sandals. The
Professor and I were seated on
Chairs near him but the others,
The devotees, sat on the ground
In a circle extending out into
The eerie dark. I felt that some
Kind of emanation was coming
From Nalanda into my own
Body, and I'd never had such
An experience before. It was
Not an unpleasant feeling. It
Was more like being a little
High on wine. I couldn't, of
Course, understand what he

Was saying, but Vivekananda
Whispered a word now and then.

I could see I was entirely out of
My depth. I'd had a course or
Two in philosophy at Harvard,
But the abstractions proposed
By Nalanda were from another
Thought-system, one for which
I was ill prepared. I caught bits
Of epistemology, whiffs of the
Philosophy of *Existenz*, but the
Frame was all alien. A different
Kind of mind, a sledgehammer
Of a mind, was at work. I gave
Up trying to understand and let
Myself drift as I watched, lost
In his gestures and intonations.

He lectured for about an hour,
Then rose to give his audience
The namaste blessing, with
Palms together, bowing in a
Circle to include everyone at
The gathering. Then came the
Gifts of food—bread, fruit, and
Vegetables laid out at his feet.
Nalanda asked Vivekananda
And me to stay on. The accent
Of his English was difficult, but
He was cordial, calling me "Mr.
Young America" with a warm
Smile. Vivekananda was well
Versed in Vedanta; they talked

For a half-hour in Malayalam;
And when it was time for us to
Go, Nalanda asked me if I had
A question. But my mind went
Blank: what could I ask of the
Great sage? He smiled and said:
"So, let *me* ask *you* a question.
In America, tell me, what do
They teach you is between two
Thoughts?" I could think of no
Answer to that. I had no answer.
"No matter," said Nalanda. "In
Time you may be ready for such
A question. But fix it in your
Mind. Do not forget it before
You are ready." And all these
Years I've remembered, though
I know I can never answer the
Question. I scarcely understand
It. And is Sri Nalanda still alive?
Wherever he may be, what is
The space between his thoughts?

On my last evening with Raja
Rao we cycled out to the beach
To watch the sunset—a good
One, the sky blazing with many
Colors. At first the setting sun
Seemed a small, distant disk,
But as darkness fell it grew and
Grew into a huge ball of fiery
Red. "That is the great god
Agni," Raja Rao told me, "the
Eternal fire. He is many things.

He is the most important of
The Vedic divinities. First, he
Is the god of the altar fire and
Its sacrifices. Then he is the
Mediator between gods and
Men. And beyond that he is the
God of lightning and the sun."

As we pedaled back through
The dark countryside toward
Trivandrum, we began to smell
The loveliest natural perfume
I've encountered anywhere in
Any country. It's the evening
Scent of India. The people in
Their huts are cooking their
Last meal of the day, using
Cow patties to fuel their fires.
Every patty the cows let fall
Is picked up and saved by the
Children. The smoke rises in
The warm night air softly. It's
A pungent smell and a little
Sweet. It's the smell of India,
Primeval India of the first
Gods and the first real people.

MELISSA

Only "pretty," not "beautiful"?
She was almost angry about my
Half compliment. We were riding
In a cab to dinner in London.
It was about our third date and
I'd been looking down the neck
Of her dress; she never wore a
Bra, she was casual about such
Conventions. Melissa was from
Australia, from a town near Perth,
But her parents had transplanted
To England when she was about ten
So she'd finished her schooling
In Sussex. She'd made the move
Early enough so she'd entirely
Lost the awful Australian accent;
Everyone took her for a Brit. But
In her personality she kept the
Australian openness and ready
Friendliness with strangers. She
Could be a good friend after a few
Conversations. Yet there was
Sensitivity and a delicacy of
Feeling in all her relationships.
No coarseness such as Australians
Sometimes have. No rough talk.
I came to understand how she was
What she was when one Sunday she
Took me down to Sussex on the
Train to meet her "Mum." A small

House on the outskirts of a
Village. Her mother was living
On a pension, the father had died
Some years back, and she'd had a
Hard time making do for two girls.

But the garden was all trim,
Weeded and the borders edged.
The house was neat as a pin.
There was a pretty tea with
Watercress sandwiches and
Scones, a tiny vase of lobelias
On the tray. Her mother was
Relaxed and well-spoken, a sense
Of humor too. No touch of
Accent. Melissa's new accent
Was a bit Clerkenwell, the part
Of London past Holborn where
She lived, a district that
Borders on the slummy: little
Tawdry shops. She'd picked up
A bit of the way they talk
There because she thought it
Funny. A little slur of cockney,
But she could get her studio
There for a very cheap rent.
Five flights of steep
Stairs up to her place, but
She'd made a bower of it,
Pretty things picked up
At auctions. Pots of flowers
And climbing vines at the
Windows. Old prints, copies
Of pictures she loved cut

From art magazines. Sonia
Delaunay was one of her loves.
Some of her own abstractions,
Straightedge drawings, lovely
Contrasts of subtle colors.
Believe this or not, she liked
To paint lying on her tummy
In the middle of the floor
With a sheet down to save
The carpet if a paint pot
Turned over. It was a hard go
With her work because she
Had no gallery though she
Sold a painting now and then
But for almost nothing. She
Made her living teaching at
The Royal College, and an
Odd job now and then at a
Shop. With her smile she
Could sell ice to the Eskimos.

The first time we made love
Was in the bracken on a bluff
Overlooking the Channel in
Dorset near an ancient village
Named Little Piddle-on-Trent.
It was warm but clouds were
Riding across the sky. The
Bracken was soft. Our loving
Was soft and slow. It always
Was that way. We could be happy
Just looking and touching and
Stroking. Her skin was so white
And perfect. I teased her that

She had the proverbial skin
Of an English dairymaid. Gray
Eyes. Long reddish hair. To
Please me she'd sometimes put
Her hair up in a braid that
Hung down her back. It was a
Bother for her, but "All right,
James, if you'll take me to
Dinner at the White Tower, I'll
Put up my hair for you, you old
Fetishist." She would gobble
Up a good meal but one of her
Specialties was Heinz's baked
Beans served cold. She had
Tiny feet and one pair of
Shoes with heels. Only one
Long dress for going out.
Mostly she wore blue jeans.
She'd never let me buy her
Any clothes except once when
We were on a lovely long
Weekend in Paris to tour the
Galleries, she weakened when
We passed a boutique on the
Rue Saint-Honoré. She found
A long swirling dress of fine
White linen which made her
Look like Joan of Arc in a
Windstorm, though when we
Went to dinner at the Grand
Véfours in the Palais Royal,
Where the other guests all
Stared at her, she looked like
A princess. Books she'd always

Let me give her. She was a big
Reader; she read much more
Than I and always good
Things. With her love she
Gave me so much more than
I could ever give her. I used
To ask her to come to America,
But she wouldn't even consider
It. "New York would kill me in
A month," she said. "You're a
Dear man, James, and I'll not
Likely ever love anyone as much
As I do you, but I'm a London
Girl, a Clerkenwell girl, and
Here's where I belong, this is
The spot for me."

BROWN

My name is Verity Jones
And I'm a second-year
Graduate student in English
At Brown. Professor Schlegel,
The head of the department,
Has eyes for me; he's just
Handed me a nice little plum
That will help with my tuition.
I'm to be teaching assistant
For a man who has no Ph.D.
Who is being imported for a term
To give a seminar on modern
Poetry, mostly Pound & Williams.
His coming is a project of our
New lady dean, who is terrific,
Everyone admires her, she's so
Liberal, wants to shake things
Up a bit. Literature she says
Should be taught with more
Than academic footnotes or
Semiotical games. She'd like
To bring in now and then people
Who've had practical experience
Working with books and writers.
This man, his name is Laughlin,
Runs the far-out avant-garde
Press New Directions. He knew
Pound & Willaims and a lot of
Other modernist poets. It sounds
As if he'll be fun to work with,

If he isn't a creep. He has
Published many of the novels
Of Jack Hawkes who's a pillar
Of the Brown department. I've
Checked with Jack who says he's
OK. He has never done any teaching
And won't have a clue as to how
A university works, but he's
An amusing talker. I'm to
Run the mechanical side of
The class and keep him from
Falling on his face with the
Students. It sounds like it
Might be fun and the money
For the job is good, I can
Use it.

EPILOGUE:
AN HONEST HEART...
A KNOWING HEAD

Thomas Jefferson counsels a student. Excerpts from a letter to Peter Carr, written in 1785.

... Time now begins to be precious
To you. Every day you lose, will
Retard a day your entrance on that
Public stage whereon you may begin
To be useful to yourself. However,
The way to repair the loss is to
Improve the future time. I trust,
That with your dispositions, even
The acquisition of science is a
Pleasing employment. I can assure
You, that the possession of it is,
What (next to an honest heart)
Will above all things render you
Dear to your friends, and give
You fame and promotion ...
Give up money, give up fame,
Give up science, give up the
Earth itself and all it contains,
Rather than do an immoral act.
And never suppose that in any
Possible situation, or under
Any circumstances, it is best
For you to do a dishonorable
Thing, however slightly so it
May appear to you. ...

From the practice of the purest
Virtue, you may be assured you
Will derive the most sublime
Comforts in every moment of
Life, and in the moment of death. . . .
An honest heart being the first
Blessing, a knowing head is the
Second. It is time for you now
To be choice in your reading;
To begin to pursue a regular
Course in it; and not to suffer
Yourself to be turned to the
Right or left by reading any
Thing out of that course. . . .

For the present, I advise you
To begin a course of antient
History, reading everything in
The original and not in translations.
First read Goldsmith's history
Of Greece. This will give you a
Digested view of that field.
Then take up antient history
In the detail, reading the
Following books in the
Following order: Herodotus,
Thucydides, Xenophontis
Hellenica, Anabasis,
Arrian, Quintus Curtius,
Diodorus Siculus, Justin.

This shall form the first
Stage of your historical
Reading, and is all I should

Mention to you now. The
Next, will be of Roman
History; Livy, Sallust,
Caesar, Cicero's epistles,
Suetonius, Tacitus, Gibbon.
From that we will come down
To modern history.

In Greek and Latin poetry,
You have read or will read
At school: Virgil, Terence,
Horace, Anacreon, Theocritus,
Homer, Euripides, Sophocles.
Read also Milton's "Paradise
Lost," Shakespeare, Ossian,
Pope's and Swift's works, in
Order to form your style in
Your own language. In
Morality, read Epictetus,
Xenophontis Memorabilia,
Plato's Socratic dialogues,
Cicero's philosophies,
Antoninus, and Seneca. . . .

Give about two hours of
Every day to exercise;
For health must not be
Sacrificed to learning. A
Strong body makes the mind
Strong. As to the species
Of exercise, I advise the
Gun. While this gives a
Moderate exercise to the
Body, it gives boldness,

Enterprise, and independence
To the mind. Games played
With the ball, and others
Of that nature, are too
Violent for the body, and
Stamp no character on the
Mind. Let your gun
Therefore be the constant
Companion of your walks.
Never think of taking a
Book with you. The object
Of walking is to relax the mind.
You should therefore not permit
Yourself even to think while you
Walk; but divert your attention
By the objects surrounding you.
Walking is the best possible
Exercise. Habituate yourself
To walk very far. The Europeans
Value themselves on having
Subdued the horse to the uses
Of man; but I doubt whether
We have not lost more than we
Have gained, by the use of
This animal. No one has
Occasioned so much, the
Degeneracy of the human
Body. An Indian goes on
Foot nearly as far in a
Day, for a long journey,
As an enfeebled white does
On his horse; and he will
Tire the best horses. . . .

You are now, I expect,
Learning French. You must
Push this; because the
Books which will be put
Into your hands when you
Advance into Mathematics,
Natural philosophy, Natural
History, etc. will be mostly
French, these sciences being
Better treated by the French
Than the English writers.
Our future connection
With Spain renders that
The most necessary of
The modern languages,
After the French. When
You become a public man,
You may have occasion
For it, and the circumstance
Of your possessing that
Language, may give you a
Preference over other
Candidates. I have
Nothing further to
Add for the present, but
Husband well your time,
Cherish your instructors,
Strive to make everybody
Your friend, and be
Assured, that nothing
Will be so pleasing
As your success, to,
Dear Peter,
Yours affectionately,
Thomas Jefferson.

NOTES AND ACKNOWLEDGMENTS

NOTES

Abbreviations for some frequently cited books:

AWCW *The Autobiography of William Carlos Williams.* New York: New Directions, 1967.

CAAS Contemporary Authors Autobiographical Series, vol. 22. Detroit, MI: Gale Research, Inc., 1996.

Cantos Ezra Pound. *The Cantos of Ezra Pound.* New York: New Directions, 1996.

CP James Laughlin. *The Collected Poems of James Laughlin.* Introduction by Hayden Carruth. Wakefield, RI, and London: Moyer Bell, 1994.

CPWCW I. The Collected Poems of William Carlos Williams, Volume I 1909–1939. Edited by A. Walton Litz and Christopher MacGowan. New York: New Directions, 1986.

CPWCW II. The Collected Poems of William Carlos Williams, Volume II 1939–1962. Edited by Christopher MacGowan. New York: New Directions, 1988.

CR James Laughlin. *The Country Road.* Cambridge, MA: Zoland Books, 1995.

PAW James Laughlin. *Pound as Wuz: Essays and Lectures on Ezra Pound by James Laughlin.* Introduction by Hugh Kenner. St. Paul, MN: Graywolf Press, 1987.

PC Ezra Pound. *The Pisan Cantos.* Edited and annotated by Richard Sieburth. New York: New Directions, 2003.

PNS James Laughlin. *Poems New and Selected.* Introduction by Charles Tomlinson. New York: New Directions, 1998.

SR James Laughlin. *The Secret Room.* New York: New Directions, 1997.

WCWJL William Carlos Williams and James Laughlin: Selected Letters. Edited by Hugh Wittemeyer. New York: W.W. Norton, 1989.

PROLOGUE—THE NORFOLK SANTA—DAWN

Collected in *CR*. An earlier version of the poem appeared in *Ambit* 131 (1993) and was reprinted *CAAS*. The principal difference between the two earlier and final versions is the classical correlative passage that begins where the present poem ends:

And as it was in Greece so long ago

Phoebus Apollo, favoured son
Of Zeus, and Eros, god of love,
Whom later times called Cupid,
Were rivals in the power
of their bows. Delian Apollo
Had struck down a great serpent,
The Python. He taunted Eros:
"What hast thou to do with the arms
Of men, thou wanton boy?" Eros,
Child of Venus, replied: "Thy dart
May pierce all things else, Apollo,
But mine shall pierce thee."
Forthwith he took from his quiver
Two arrows of opposite effect:
One blunt and tipped with lead
Puts to flight; the other sharp
And tipped with shining gold
Kindles the flames of love.
With the golden dart Eros pierced
The flesh of Apollo, pierced even
Into the bone and marrow. Straightway
Apollo burned with love. With the lead
Arrow Eros wounded the fair-formed
Daphne, a sweet nymph of the forest
Glades whose father was Peneus,
The river god. She hated the very name

Of love, rejoicing in the deep fastnesses
Of the woods and in the spoils of beasts
Which she had snared. A single fillet
Bound her locks all unarranged.
Her father rebuked her, pleading
For grandsons. O father dearest,
Grant me to enjoy perpetual virginity,
As you have done for Diana, the huntress.
But Daphne's beauty is irresistible.
Apollo loves her at sight and
Longs to wed her. He gazes at her eyes,
Gleaming like stars. He gazes
At her lips, which but to gaze on
Does not satisfy. He marvels at
Her fingers, hands and wrists,
And her arms bare to the shoulders,
And what is hid he deems still lovelier.
But Daphne flees him swifter than
The fleeting breeze. So does the lamb
Flee from the wolf, the deer
From the lion. "Nay, stay," Apollo
Cries, "Learn who thy lover is.
I am no unkempt guardian of
Flocks and herds. Mine is the Delphian
Land; Zeus is my father. By me
The Lyre responds in harmony to song.
The art of medicine is my discovery.
Alas, that love is curable
By no herbs." But the maiden
Pursues her frightened way, even in
Her desertion seeming fair.
The winds bare her limbs;
The opposing breezes set her
Garments aflutter as she runs;
But the chase draws to an end

For the youthful god would no longer
Waste his time in coaxing words.
So run the god and maid, he sped
By hope and she by fear.

Now is her strength all gone,
And she cries out to Peneus, her father:
"O father, help! If your waters hold
Divinity, change and destroy this beauty
By which I please o'er well."
Scarce had she made this prayer
When a down-dragging numbness
Seized her limbs and her soft sides
Were begirt with thin bark. Her hair
Was changed to leaves; her arms to
Branches. Her feet but now so swift,
Grew fast in sluggish roots, and her head
Was now but a tree's top. Her gleaming
Beauty alone remained. But even so
In this new form Apollo loved her,
And placing his hand upon the trunk
He felt the heart still fluttering
Beneath the bark. He embraced the
Branches as if human limbs and pressed
His lips upon the wood. But even
The wood shrank from his kisses.
And the god cried out to her:
"Since thou canst not be my bride,
Thou shalt at least be my tree. My
Hair, my lyre, my quiver shall always
Be entwined with thee. With thee shall
Roman generals wreathe their heads
When shouts of joy shall acclaim
Their triumph, and long processions
Climb the Capitol.

A marginal gloss in *Ambit* reads: *"Ovid: 'Metamorphoses,' Book I / the Translation of F.J. Miller / in the Loeb Library / Much abridged"*

p. 1. **The Dragon and the Unicorn.** By Kenneth Rexroth, first published by New Directions in 1952 and later included in *The Collected Longer Poems of Kenneth Rexroth* (New Directions, 1968).

p. 2. **Cranky Old Bear.** See below, p. 215, "The Old Bear: Kenneth Rexroth." **dove sta memoria.** From Guido Cavalcanti's *Canzone* (*"Donna me priegha"*), *"In quella parte / dove sta memoria,"* translated by Ezra Pound in his Canto 36 as, "Where memory liveth / it takes its state," reversing the order of the lines.

p. 3. **That year when I lived in Burma.** The year was 1957.

p. 4. **Ne quid nimis.** Latin; literally, "Nothing too much."

p. 6. **the Kyprian herself.** Footnoted in *CR*: *"Aphrodite was born on Cyprus."*

THE ANCESTORS

Collected in *CR* and first published in *CAAS*.

p. 9. **And when we finally / made it to Portaferry.** In 1983, JL and his wife Ann—in England with the filmmaker Lawrence Pitkethly for the shooting of a documentary on Ezra Pound for public television—made a trip to Northern Ireland. **1824.** Another possible date is 1827. **Alexander and / James . . .** James Laughlin II (1806–82). **Joyce.** I.e., James Joyce.

p. 10. Photograph: JL's great-grandfather, James Laughlin II. **His son James.** JL's grandfather (1847–1923).

p. 11. Photograph: JL's grandfather, James Laughlin, Jr.

p. 12. **Henry, my father.** Henry Hughart Laughlin (1878–1938). **another Henry.** Henry Laughlin, a cousin of JL's father, became president of Houghton Mifflin.

MY SHOELACES

Collected in *SR*. First publishd in *Ambit* 139 (1995) as part I of "Two Views of London," which was reprinted in *CAAS*.

p. 15. Photograph: JL age ten, 1924.

p. 16. **my brother.** Henry Hughart Laughlin, Jr. (1909–84).

MY PATERNAL GRANDMOTHER

Previously un published.

p. 19. **Danny.** Sidney Ford Page (1838–1925), known as Danny, was married to JL's grandfather, James Laughlin, Jr. Photograph: JL and his grandmother Danny at Sydonie, the Laughlin winter home in Zellwood, FL.

p. 22. **The Burns / Poem on Bannockburn.** JL quotes the first three of the poem's six stanzas.

ARE WE TOO OLD TO MAKE LOVE?

Collected in *CR* and first published in *CAAS*.

p. 25. **Some fifty years ago … / … I was seventeen.** The year may have been 1934, when JL was in fact nineteen years old.

HARVARD—BOSTON—RAPALLO

Originally titled "Harvard—Boston." The opening section, pp. 29–40, first appeared in *Ambit* 147 (1997) with the chronological-ly misleading title, "Harvard, Fair Harvard 1934–35," and the seg-ment "The Aftermath" (p. 74) in *Ambit* 150 (1997). "Ezra (Pound)" (p. 83) was collected in *CR*, originally published in *Ambit* 132 (1993), and reprinted in *CAAS*. The following section titles are editorial additions and are not in the original manuscripts: "Father" (p. 64), "Daphne" (p. 87), "T.S. Eliot" (p. 94), "Pornography at Harvard" (p. 95), "Skiing" (p. 97), "Rapallo Again" (p. 100), "Austria" (p. 115).

p. 30. Photograph of JL's father, Henry Hughart Laughlin, by Strickler.

p. 31. **Choate.** JL entered The Choate School, Wallingford, CT, in 1929 and graduated in 1932.

p. 36. **"Frisky" Merriman.** Roger Bigelow "Frisky" Merriman, Harvard '96, was the first master (1931–42) of Eliot House.

p. 41. **"Canned beer."** JL remembers the convivial spirit of the *Advocate* office in early 1933 though not the letter. The first beer cans, for Krueger's beer, came on the market in January 1935.

p. 43. **Colonel Apted.** Head of the Harvard campus police.

p. 44. **Le Rosey.** JL attended Le Rosey, at Rolle on Lake Geneva, in 1927.

p. 45. **Gordon Cairnie.** Proprietor of the Grolier Book Shop in Cambridge, which he founded in 1927.

p. 46. **"Melcarth."** Perhaps JL is in fact thinking of Charles Robert Maturin's *Melmoth the Wanderer* (1820).

p. 47. **Joe's grandfather...the Pulitzer / Prize.** The elder Joseph Pulitzer (d. 1911) never received one of his Pulitzer Prizes, which were established in 1917 at his bequest.

p. 53. **Est amare dulce / in juventute.** Latin: "Sweet it is to love in youth." The words are almost certainly of JL's composition. His original manuscript reads *dulcis* for *dulce*, an error that he would surely have corrected had it been pointed out to him.

p. 57. **Ted Spencer.** JL in fact did not return to the subject of Theodore Spencer in *Byways*. New Directions published his book of poems, *The Paradox in the Circle*, in 1941, and he contributed the introduction to ND's edition of James Joyce's *Stephen Hero* (1944, 1963).

p. 58. **Unsere ganze Philosophie. . . .** More correctly, "All our philosophy. . . ." The original manuscript, uncorrected, reads: *"Unser ganze Philosophie / ist eine Berichtigung der Sprachgebrauch."*

p. 59–60. **God as inter- / dependent from the world.** With better sense, "interdependent with the world."

pp. 60. **"Matty" Matthiesen....*Selected Poems* of Melville.**

Melville's *Selected Poems*, with F.O. Matthiesen's introduction, was published by ND in 1944.

p. 61. **Professor / Pease . . . president of Amherst.** Arthur Pease was president of Amherst College, Amherst, MA, from 1927 to 1932.

p. 62. **Des jeunes filles / Bien élevées en fleur.** French, "Some well-bred young girls in bloom." The allusion here is to the title of part two of Marcel Proust's *Remembrance of Things Past*: *A l'ombre des jeunes en fleur*, translated by Scott Montcrieff as *Within a Budding Grove*.

p. 65. **he resigned from / The company.** The year was 1923.

p. 66. **Bob Stupple.** Stupple, a professional competitor, was later a runner-up to Al Watrous in the 1957 PGA Seniors' Championship.

p. 68. **Madame de Hauteville.** Or Geneviève de Hautecoeur. See below, p. 77. Photograph of JL's mother, Margery Rea Laughlin, by Bachrach, 1941.

p. 71. **Great-aunt Edith, daughter of the Pittsburgh man.** Very likely Edith Oliver, who married JL's mother's brother, Robinson Rea.

p. 74. **the next / Summer . . . Heathrow.** Perhaps 1929. There is a chronology problem in "The Aftermath," which clearly follows JL's previous reminiscences about his father, on pp. 64–74, and even elaborates on them. It seems clear that JL traveled from the United States to England to meet his father. However, he would have had to have gone by boat, since commercial transatlantic flights began in 1939, the year after JL's father's death, while London's Heathrow Airport was not opened until 1946.

p. 77. **Geneviève de Hautecoeur.** No doubt the Madame de Hauteville of the previous section, p. 68, so that one or another is a fictitious name, if not both.

p. 81. **Woodland Road house.** The address of JL's family's home in Pittsburgh was 104 Woodland Road.

pp. 83–87. **Ezra (Pound).** For another account of JL's first extended stay in Rapallo, see *PAW*, pp. 3–10. The version of this section published in *Ambit* was preceded by two correlatives, the first of JL's composition in the metrical style of *Byways*, the second derived from St. Augustine. It was followed by three classical correlatives, the first two playing off of Pound's "Homage to Sextus Propertius" and the final one reworked from Martial.

> *'When I was a boy with never a crack in my heart'*
> —*Yeats, "The Meditation of the Old Fisherman*
> I roamed all roads,
> Hungering to find out
> What they meant when they spoke
> Of love. I was holding my heart
> In my hand, offering it to anyone
> Who would take it.
> She who was the first
> Was older than I.
> She knew men and their ways.
> She had suffered from some
> Who threw her away
> After their amusement.
> Now she was seeking an innocent
> Whom she could shape to her pleasing.
> I will not condemn her;
> She taught me so much I had to learn
> One way or another
> But I began to fear her,
> Beautiful and passionate as she was.
> I knew she would alter me in ways
> I didn't want to accept.
> It was only a matter of time
> Till she had incised a crack
> In my heart, a crack that
> Would not quickly heal.
> So I went my way;
> I took to the road again, looking
> For another less demanding.

[Marginal gloss: *"St. Augustine: / The Confessions, / Book Three / The William Watts / translation in / the Loeb Library"*]

Carthage St. Augustine

*Veni Karthaginem, et circumstrepebat
me undique sartago flagitiosorum amorum.*

To Carthage then I came, where
A whole frying-pan full of abominable
Loves crackled around me and on
Every side. I sought about for
Something to love, loving still
To be in love: security too
I hated and that way too that had
No snares in it: and all because
I had a famine within me, even of
That inward food (thyself O God)
Though that famine made me not
Hungry. For I continued without
All appetite towards incorruptible
Nourishments, not because I was
Already full, but the more empty,
The more queasy stomached. For this
Cause my soul was not very well,
But miserably breaking out into
Botches, had an extreme itch to be
Scratched by the touch of these
Sensible things, which yet if they
Had not a life, would not be
Loved at all. It was very pleasurable
To me, both to love, and to be loved;
But much more, when I obtained
To enjoy the person whom I enjoyed.
I defiled therefore the spring of

Friendship with the filth of
Uncleanliness, and I besullied
The purity of it with the hell of
Lustfulness. But thus filthy and
Dishonest, with a superlative kind
Of vanity I took pride to pass
For a spruce and gentle companion.
I forced myself also into love,
With which I affected to be
Ensnared. My God, My Mercy, with
How much sourness didst thou of
Thy goodness to me, besour that
Sweetness? For obtaining once
To be beloved again, and secretly
Arriving to the bond of enjoying:
I was with much joy bound with
Sorrow-bringing embracements,
Even that I might be scourged
With the iron burning rods of
Jealousy, and suspicion, and
Fears, and angers, and brawls.

[Marginal gloss: *"Propertius Recreatus / Some lines from Pound's* **Homage**"]

What foot beat out your time-bar,
    what water has mellowed your whistle?

[Marginal gloss: "*(Correlative)*"]

And in the meantime my songs will travel,
    And the devirginated young ladies will
    enjoy them
    When they have got over their strangeness,

My cellar does not date from Numa Pompilius,
    Nor bristle with wine jars,
    Nor is it equipped with a frigidaire
    patent;

If she goes in a gleam of Cos, in a slither
    of dyed stuff,
There is a volume in the matter;

And my ventricles do not palpitate to
    Caesarial *ore rotundos*,

It is noble to die of love, and honorable
    to remain uncuckolded for a season.

Such derelictions have destroyed other
    young ladies aforetime,
And what they swore in the cupboard
    wind and wave have scattered away.

There are enough women in hell,
    quite enough beautiful women,

You are a very early inspector of
    mistresses.
Do you think I have adopted your
    habits?

Zeus' clever rapes, in the old days.

Of all these young women
    not one had enquired the cause of
    the world.

[Marginal gloss: *"Martial: Introduction / to the Epigrams. A very / free adaptation, based / on the translation of Walter C.A. Ker. (Correlative)"*]

I hope that in my books I have
Followed a middle course so that
No right-thinking reader can complain
Of them. I hope their liveliness
Does not put anyone, even unimportant
People, in a bad light. I trust I
Have not maltreated the writers
Who have gone before me, or misspelled
Their names. If fame comes to me,
May it be without cost to anyone
Else. And may it not come simply
From cleverness. Let there be no
Malicious interpretation of my
Jokes, such as they are. Let me
Not be rewritten for the amusement
Of those who come after me. No
Censorship please. I realize that
I have expressed myself very freely,
Both in what I say and how I say it.
Is that not my privilege as a poet?
If there are any prudish readers
Who think I have no right to talk
In plain English let them try to
Be satisfied with this apology.
I beg of you the credit for my work
That is seldom given to poets
While they are still alive.

p. 85. **i mercanti di cannoni.** Italian: "the arms merchants."
Dromena . . . epopteia. Ancient Greek. *Dromena* refers to
the mystical rites of the Eleusinian mysteries and *epopteia* to
the highest stage of initiation in them. **salite.** Italian: the stony
"slopes" behind Rapallo. *"Micci, micci, / Vieni qua. . . ."*
Italian: "Kitty, kitty, / Come here. . . . "

p. 86. **Gaudier.** The French sculptor Henri Gaudier-Breska
(1891–1915). Pound's memoir *Gaudier-Breska* was first published in 1916 and reissued by ND in 1961.

p. 87. **Daughter.** Pound's daughter, Mary de Rachewiltz. *Great Learning . . . Odes.* Pound's translation of "The Great Learning," retitled "The Great Digest," was published by ND in his *Confucius* in 1951 and his translations of *The Confucian Odes* in 1954.

p. 90. **My cousin Duncan Phillips.** In 1921 Duncan Phillips (1886–1967) founded the The Phillips Collection, the famed museum of modern art in Washington, D. C. **book on the Renaissance.** JL is probably thinking of *The Leadership of Giorgione* (1937), though it was published two years after his romance with Daphne.

pp. 94–95. **T.S. Eliot's residency . . . Bill Williams.** T.S. Eliot delivered the Charles Eliot Norton Lectures at Harvard in 1932–33, while JL began his correspondence with W.C. Williams in December 1933, after he had been elected to the editorial board of the *Advocate*, so the events described here belong, technically speaking, earlier in the the narrative of the section "Harvard—Boston—Rapallo." However, JL writes elsewhere in *Byways* (p. 155) that Williams "hated / T. S. Eliot (whom he never / Met . . . .

p. 99. **Erling Strom.** Strom (b. 1897), who emigrated to the United States in 1919, was a pioneer in sports skiing in North America. He ran lodges in Stowe, VT, and at Mt. Assiniboine, BC, and participated in the first ski ascent of Mt. McKinley in 1932.

p. 101. **"Stele."** The poem is section VI of "Moeurs Contemporaines."

p. 103. **"Albuggero Rapallo."** Pound's name for the Albergo Rapallo. The Pounds ate at the hotel because Dorothy did not cook. See *PAW*, pp. 3–4. **monolithic . . . Gaudier.** The marble *Hieratic Head of Ezra Pound.* See Pound, *Gaudier-Brzeska*, plates XIII and XXIX.

p. 106. **"In Another Country."** A bilingual poem, in English and Italian; the title piece of a selection of JL's poems published by City Lights Books in 1978 and later included in *CP. Noctes*

incredibiles. Latin: "Incredible nights." ***topolino.*** Italian: "small automobile."

p. 107. ***autostrade.*** Italian: "highways."

pp. 108–113. **Tempio Malatestiano . . . Federigo da Montefeltro . . . Sigismundo Pandolfo Malatesta**, etc. See Pound's "Renaissance Cantos" (Cantos VIII-XI), which revolve around the central figure of Malatesta. According to JL, Pound indentified Mussolini with Malatesta, "one of his great heroes of the Renaissance" (*PAW*, p. 20).

p. 113. ***Tempus Loquendi Tempus Tacendi.*** The actual Latin text of the Vulgate (Ecclesiastes 3:7) reads, "*tempus tacendi et tempus loquendi.*" **San Vitale**. A Byzantine church in Ravenna, built in 526–27.

p. 116. ***Geburtshaus.*** German: "birthplace." **Nansen Passport.** More accurately, "Nansen Certificate," a document issued to postwar refugees who were without identity papers. The certificates were named after the former arctic explorer Fridtjof Nansen (1861–1930), the League of Nations high commissioner for refugees, who was awarded the 1920 Nobel Peace Prize for his work. **wealth . . . swallowed by the Communists.** In the period JL is referring to, during the breakup of the old Austro-Hungarian empire, Transylvania was ceded by Hungary to Romania. It was in fact the monarchical government that expropriated the estates of wealthy ethnic Hungarians and redistributed them to Romanian peasants. The later Communist expropriations followed World War II.

pp. 118–21. **Koos Vanderleou.** JL is possibly confounding the story of Koos Vanderleou with that of J.J. van der Leeuw, the Dutch theosophist who was in analysis with Freud in 1933 and died the following year while piloting his airplane over Tanganyika. If so, the episode recounted here may have taken place in 1933–34. JL's travels in Europe during the 1930s, in the summers and while on leaves from Harvard, were more frequent and extensive than he recalls in *Byways*. **Berggasse.** Freud's home and office in Vienna were located at Berggasse 19.

p. 122. *Kaiserschmarren* (a sweet omelet). In fact, a pancake sweetened with sugar and raisins, named after Empress (German: *Kaiserin*) Elizabeth of Austria (1837–98).

p. 123. *Matratzenlager.* Simply a place where mattressses are thrown down for the night.

p. 125. *Zwei Groschen* poker. German: "two-penny ante" poker.

p. 126. **Gerhart Münch.** Münch (1907–88) made the violin arrangement of the French Renaissance composer Clément Jannequin's "Le Chant des Oiseaux" that comprises Pound's Canto LXXV. **the concerts Ezra sponsored in the *municipio*.** Between 1933 and 1939 Pound organized a series of occasional concerts in Rapallo's town hall (*municipio*), with Olga Rudge and Gerhart Münch as its principal players. **"*Weisst du . . . Besitztum Ezras ist?*"** The uncorrected German in the original manuscript reads: "*Weist du / Nicht dass diese Dame ist die / Besitztum Ezras?*"

p. 127. **Sant' Ambrogio.** A village in the hills above Rapallo.

p. 128. *Schwundgeld.* "Pound," writes Richard Sieburth, "was a proponent of the stamp scrip introduced in the Austrian town of Wörgl, which he visited in 1935. Called *Schwundgeld* or 'disappearing money,' this locally issued currency lost its value if not spent within a certain period of time—an incentive against hoarding of money, designed to increase the circulation of goods and services." *PC*, p. 127.

p. 129. **the Salute.** The church of Santa Maria della Salute on the Grand Canal.

p. 130. **Count Chigi Saracini . . . gave Olga a nice position.** At this time, Olga Rudge was Secretary to the Accademia Musicale Chigiana in Siena. **Monte dei Paschi . . . Duke Leopold of Siena had founded.** The year was 1472.

pp. 131–32. **a surprise Visit in New York from Olga and Ezra.** The date was Sunday, June 4, 1967. For another account by JL of Pound's 1967 visit to the United States (where he gives the year as 1969), see *PAW*, pp. 30–31. **our apartment in the Village.** JL and his wife Ann kept a *pied-à-terre* at 9

Bank Street in Greenwich Village, not far from the New York office of New Directions. **the annual meeting of The Academy of American Poets.** On June 5, 1967. **Norfolk.** JL's home and his private New Directions office outside of New York City were in Norfolk, CT.

p. 132. **the Last of the *Cantos*.** JL quotes from "Fragment (1966)," which is placed at the very end of Pound's complete *Cantos* and concludes with:

> These lines are for the
> ultimate CANTO

> whatever I may write
> in the interim.

> [24 *August* 1966]

MY AUNT

Collected in *CP*, first published in *Ambit* 134 (1994), and reprinted in *CAAS*. The *Ambit* version includes a final stanza that acts as a bridge to an accompanying classical correlative paraphrasing Marcus Aurelius.

> Marcus Aurelius

> When she was in her early twenties
> my aunt became interested in book-
> binding. With her typical determi-
> nation she went to London, took a
> flat with a chaperone and studied
> binding in the atelier of Cobden-
> Sanderson at the Doves Press. She
> did some lovely little volumes
> bound in fine skins of Morocco

and decorated with imaginative
gold tooling. One of the most
handsome was a *Meditations* of
Marcus Aurelius. When she gave it
to me she adjured me to study the
contents. My aunt was not a student of philosophy but in her
way she was a Stoic. As I read the
text now I recognize so much of
her spirit in its morality and
wisdom.

[Marginal gloss: "MARCUS AURELIUS ANTONINUS / EMPEROR OF
ROME A.D. 161–80 / THE MEDITATIONS / (Translation of G.H.
Reendall / Excerpts from Book II)

When you wake, say to yourself:
Today I shall encounter meddling,
ingratitude, violence, cunning,
jealousy, self-seeking; all of
them the results of men not knowing
what is good and what is evil. But
seeing that I have beheld the
nature and nobility of good, and
the nature and meanness of evil . . .
I cannot be injured by any of them;
for no man can involve me in what
demeans. Neither can I be angry
with my brother, or quarrel with
him; for we are made for cooper-
ation, like the feet, the hands,
the eyelids, the upper and the
lower rows of teeth . . . Whatever
you do or say or think, it is in
your power, remember, to take

leave of life. In departing from
this world, if indeed there are
gods, there is nothing to be
afraid of; for gods will not let
you fall into evil. But if there
are no gods, or if they do not
concern themselves with men, why
live on in a world devoid of gods,
or devoid of providence? But there
do exist gods, who do concern
themselves with men. And they have
put it wholly in the power of man
not to fall into any true evil . . .

By mind-power we apprehend how
quickly all things vanish, bodies
in the material world, their memories in the lapse of time: we
understand the nature of all things
of sense, particularly those which
decoy us with the bait of pleasure,
or terrify us with the threat of
pain, or are dinned into our ears
by self-conceit; how cheap they
are and despicable, filthy, perish-
able, dead. Mind sees the worth of
those whose views and voices bestow
repute; it teaches the nature of
death, and shows that anyone who
looks at it fairly in the face . . .
will come to regard it simply as
an act of nature; and none but a
child is terrified at that.
In man's life, time is but a
moment; being, a flux; sense

is dim; the material frame
corruptible; soul, an eddy of
breath; fortune a thing inscrut-
able, and fame precarious. Things
of the body are but a stream
that flows, things of the soul
a dream and vapor; life a war-
fare and a sojourning; and after
fame, oblivion. What then can
direct our goings? One thing and
one alone, philosophy; which is,
to keep the deity within invio-
late and free from scathe, superior
to pleasures and to pains,
doing nothing at random, nothing
falsely or disingenuously, and
lacking for nought, whatever
others do or leave undone; accepting the apportioned lot, as
coming from the same source as
man himself; and finally, in all
serenity awaiting death, the
natural dissolution of the elements of which each creature is
compounded. And if the component
elements have nought to fear in
the continuous change from form
to form, why should one eye look
askance at the change and dissolution of the whole? It is of
nature; and nature knows no
evil.

p. 134. **My Aunt . . . Robin Hill.** Leila Laughlin Carlisle (d. 1962).
Robin Hill was the name of her estate in Norfolk, CT. **My**

first marriage. JL was married to Margaret Keyser, of Salt Lake City, from 1942 to 1952.

p. 135. Photograph: JL's aunt Leila Laughlin Carlisle.

p. 137. **"Sydonie."** The Laughlins established their winter home, Sydonie, in 1883. **Sydney Page.** See "My Paternal Grandmother," p. 19.

p. 138. **her consort.** Leila Laughlin was married to G. Lister Carlisle at Sydonie in 1916. *sans peur et sans reproche.* French: "without fear and without reproach," traditional knightly virtues.

p.139. Photograph: The wedding of Leila Laughlin to G. Lister Carlisle. At the center, the bride and groom, with JL's older brother, Henry, in front of them. To their left, the bride's parents (JL's grandfather James and grandmother Danny) and just behind them, JL's mother, Margery; to their right, the groom's parents. At the rear center, JL's father, Henry.

REMEMBERING WILLIAM CARLOS WILLIAMS

Published as a New Directions Paperbook Original in 1994. That same year the text of pages 143–71 as they exist in the present edition appeared in *Ambit* 137 and 138, but without accompanying illustrations.

p. 142. Photograph: William Carlos Williams by Charles Sheeler.

p. 143. Photograph: young Dr. Williams.

p. 144. *Kora in Hell* **and** *Spring and All.* *Kora in Hell: Improvisations* (Boston: Four Seasons Company, 1920) and *Spring and All* (Paris: Contact Publishing Company, 1923) were eventually published by ND in Williams' *Imaginations* in 1970. *Spring and All* is also included in *CPWCW I.*

p. 146. *Poems of 1909.* Rutherford, NJ: 1909. Privately printed and never republished. *Al Que Quiere!* Boston: Four Seasons Company, 1917. *The Great American Novel.* Paris: Contact Publishing Company, 1923. *Voyage to Pagany*. New York: The Macauley Company, 1928. Reissued by ND, with an

introduction by Harry Levin, in 1970. ***White Mule.*** The book
design for ND's first edition was by Sherry Mangan.

p. 147. Photograph by Polly Storey of JL in the New Directions
office on his aunt Leila's estate in Norfolk, CT, 1939.

p. 148. **"Dear God . . . . "** For the full text of this letter, see
WCWJL, p. 5. ***The Locust Tree in Flower.*** First collected in
Williams' *An Early Martyr and Other Poems* (New York: The
Alcestis Press, 1935). See *WCWCP I*, p. 366.

pp. 149–50. ***Life Along the Passaic River.*** 1938. ***Collected Poems.***
*The Complete Collected Poems of William Carlos Williams,
1906–1938.* 1938. ***locus mirabilis.*** Latin: "wonderful place."

pp. 149–50. ***Perpetuum Mobile: The City.*** First collected in
Williams' *Adam and Eve & The City* (Peru, VT: The Alcestis
Press, 1936). See *WCWCP I*, p. 430.

pp. 150–51. ***Complaint.*** First collected in Williams' *Sour Grapes*
(Boston: Four Seasons Company, 1921). **"Of Medicine and
Poetry" in his *Autobiography*.** JL excerpts and paraphrases
various sentences from the four-page chapter. The actual text
reads: "When they ask me, as of late they frequently do, how I
have for so many years continued an equal interest in medicine and the poem, I reply that they amount for me to nearly the same thing . . . . The cured man, I want to say, is no different from any other. It is a trivial business unless you add the
zest, whatever that is, to the picture. That's how I came to find
writing such a necessity . . . . my 'medicine' was the thing
which gained me entrance to these secret gardens of the self
. . . . I was permitted by my medical badge to follow the poor,
defeated body into those gulfs and grottos . . . . just there, the
thing, in all its greatest beauty, may for a moment be freed to
fly for a moment about the room . . . . for a split second—from
one side or the other, it has fluttered before me for a moment,
a phrase which I quickly write down on anything at hand, any
piece of paper I can grab." *AWCW*, pp. 286-89.

p. 152. **"Asphodel, That Greeny Flower."** First published in
Williams' *Journey to Love* (New York: Random House, 1955)

and later included in the posthumous *Pictures from Brueghel* (Norfolk, CT: New Directions, 1963). JL quotes from the poem's concluding lines. See *WCWCP II*, p. 310.

pp. 152–53. **Many Loves . . . A Dream of Love.** *Many Loves and Other Plays* (Norfolk, CT: New Directions, 1961). JL extracts and paraphrases from *A Dream of Love*; see pp. 84 and 200–9.

p. 154. **This Is Just to Say . . . And Floss's reply.** "This Is Just to Say" was first collected in Williams' *Collected Poems 1921–31* (New York: The Objectivist Press, 1934). Floss's "Reply" was found in typescript among the Williams' papers at the State University of New York–Buffalo. See *WCWCP I*, pp. 372 and 536.

p. 155. **The Waste Land . . . wiped out our world. . . .** *AWCW,* p. 174.

p. 156. **I Wanted to Write a Poem.** *I Wanted to Write a Poem: An Autobiography of the Work of a Poet*, edited by Edith Heal (Boston: Beacon Press, 1958; reissued by ND, 1978), pp. 71–73.

p. 158. **Found notes for more pages.** "Book VI (c. 1961)" is included as an appendix to the revised edition of *Paterson* (ND, 1992), edited by Christopher MacGowan, the edition quoted in *Byways.* **Letter from WCW to JL, 1943.** December 7, 1943. For the full text, see *WCWJL*, pp. 95-96. **And another in November 1943.** For the full text, see *WCWJL*, pp. 166–68.

p. 162. **From WCW to Parker Tyler, 1948.** For the full text, see *The Selected Letters of William Carlos Williams*, edited by John C. Thirwall (New York: McDowell, Oblensky, 1957; reissued by ND, 1984). *I Wanted to Write a Poem*, p. 73.

pp. 163–64. **Marcia Nardi.** 1901–90. "some of the / Best writings. . . ." *Paterson*, p. 254n. **Nardi's poems / In our New Directions annual.** *New Directions in Prose & Poetry* 7 (1942), pp. 413–28.

pp. 164. **Excerpt from a letter to Nardi . . . .Elizabeth O'Neil**. See *The Last Word: The Letters of Marcia Nardi and William Carlos Williams*, edited by Marcia O'Neil (Iowa City:

University of Iowa Press, 1994). **From a Marcia Nardi letter.** *Paterson*, Book Two, p. 87.

p. 165. *polumetis.* Greek, epithet of Odysseus: "of many devices."

p. 166. **"The Language . . . courage to use them."** *Paterson*, Book One, p. 11. *"nihil intellectu quod non / Prius in sensu.* Latin: "There is nothing in the mind that is not first in the senses."

p. 167. **David McDowell.** 1918–85. See below, pp. 173–81. Illustration: book design by Peter Beilenson. **the ski resort in Utah.** In 1939 JL founded the Alta Lodge in Utah's Wasatch Range. **The summer . . . cottage in Norfolk.** August 1938.

pp. 167–69. **Charlottesville. . . ."Social Credit as Anti-Communism."** Williams spoke on July 10, 1936.

p. 168. *In the American Grain.* New York: Albert & Charles Boni, 1925; reissued by ND in 1939 with an introduction by Horace Gregory. "To Elsie. . . ." First published in *Spring and All.* See *CPWCW I*, p. 217.

p. 169. **"The Constitution says. . . ."** *Paterson*, p. 180. Illustration: drawing of the Passaic Falls, by Earl Horter. Illustration: *The Farmers' Daughters* (1961), photograph by Eve Arnold, cover design by Gilda Rosenblum.

p. 170. **Merrill Moore.** 1903–57. His "Six Sonnets" were included in the second ND annual, *New Directions in Prose & Poetry 1937*, and in 1938 Williams contributed a preface to Moore's *Sonnets from New Directions*, the second number in a New Directions Pamphlets series.

p. 171. **His mother, Elena Hoheb.** Raquel Hélène Rose Hoheb Williams, 1856–1949. *Yes, Mrs. Williams. Yes, Mrs. Williams: A Personal Record of My Mother* (New York: McDowell, Oblensky, 1959; reissued by ND in 1982 with a foreword by William Eric Williams). **She died at the age of 102.** Mrs. Williams died in October 1949, two and half months short of ninety-three. Photograph: Williams' mother, *c.* 1940.

p. 172. **'Smell!'** First collected in *Al Que Quiere!*

pp. 176–78. For the full texts of the letters between JL and Williams, see *WCWJL*, pp. 180–84 and 185–86.

p. 178. **Kaplan.** Maurice Serle Kaplan (d. 1951), a book designer for ND.

p. 180. **Bob MacGregor.** Robert M. MacGregor, 1911–74. **International Publications.** From 1952 to 1957, JL was president of International Publications, which published simultaneously in English, French, German, and Italian the quarterly magazine *Perspectives USA* and similar journals devoted to contemporary literature and art (e.g. below, p. 181, *Perspectives of Burma*).

p. 181. **Daw Khin Myo Chit.** Burmese writer, b. 1915.

p.182. *Mea culpa.* Latin: admission of error, literally, "through my fault." Illustration: cover photograph of Williams by Irving Wellcome, design by Gertrude Huston.

p. 183. Illustration: *Something to Say* (ND, 1985), cover drawing of Williams by Ben Shahn, design by Hermann Strohbach.

pp. 183–87. **"A Visit."** The story, which JL excerpts here, is based on a visit by him to Williams on July 1, 1960. It first appeared in the *William Carlos Williams Newsletter 4*, No. 1 (Spring 1978), was reprinted in *WCWJL*, and collected in JL's *Random Stories* (Mount Kisco, NY, and London: Moyer Bell Limited, 1990). JL made some small changes in the text for the 1995 book edition of "Remembering William Carlos Williams," so that the shortened story would stand well on its own. p. 186. **. . . these kids these new young poets, they know . . . .** Original text: "But these kids know . . . ." p. 187. **I can hardly talk. . . .** Original text: "I can't talk. . . ." p. 188. **Evans was startled . . . .but then he understood. . . .** Original text: "Evans was startled. . . .but then he took it all in . . . ."

pp. 188–89. **Bill's strokes . . . the / First in 1947.** Williams' first stroke in fact occurred four years later, in October 1951. Photograph: Williams' house at 9 Ridge Road, Rutherford, NJ.

p. 190. Photograph: Williams and Floss, March 1961. **His sons, Bill Jr. / And Paul.** William Eric Williams, 1914–95. Paul Herman Williams, 1916–2003.

p. 191. **He was in bed . . . Charles Abbott. . . .** Williams suffered a second stroke in August 1952 while visiting the home of Charles Abbott (1900–61) in Buffalo. **a nutty poem . . . Chickens.** "The Red Wheelbarrow." First published in *Spring and All*. See *CPWCW I*, p. 224. Photograph of Williams, by Tram, *c.* 1963.

p. 192. **His appointment . . . slickly aborted.** Williams' taking up his appointment at the Library of Congress for 1952–53 was delayed by the false accusation that he was a Communist, made by a certain Virginia Kent Cummins, publisher of the small magazine *Lyric*. By the time Williams' name was cleared, the term of his appointment had passed.

p. 193. **The Revelation.** First collected in Williams' *Collected Poems 1921–31*. See *CPWCW I*, p. 39.

p. 194. **"Asphodel, That Greeny Flower,"** etc. JL here quotes from the poem's opening lines. *CPWCW II*, p. 310.

p. 195. Photograph of Williams by JL. **"Bill was convinced," writes / Herbert Leibowitz. . . . A stable foot."** JL is quoting from his private correspondence with the critic Herbert Leibowitz.

pp.196–98. **Richard Eberhart . . . John Thirwall.** Richard Eberhart (b. 1904). His *Selected Poems 1930–1965* (New York: New Directions, 1965) won the Pulitzer Prize for poetry in 1966. John C. Thirwall (1904–71) edited *The Selected Letters of William Carlos Williams* (New York: McDowell, Oblensky, 1957; reissued by ND, 1984). See pp. 321, 325–26, and 331–32 for the full texts of the letters quoted here.

p. 198. **the lines in "Asphodel, / That Greeny Flower."** See *CPWCW II*, pp. 323–24.

p. 199. **"Some Simple Measures in the / American Idiom and the Variable / Foot."** See *WCWCP II*, pp. 418–23.

p. 200. **Paul Mariani. . . . extreme dejection."** Paul Mariani recounts the episode, which took place on July 30, 1960, in his biography *William Carlos Williams: A New World Naked* (New York: W.W. Norton, 1981), p. 758.

p. 202. Photograph: Williams at 9 Ridge Road.

p. 203. **Dear Jim. . . . Bill.** *WCWJL*, p. 252.

pp. 205–7. *Tract.* First collected in *Al Que Quieri!* (Boston: Four Seasons Company, 1917). See *CPWCW I*, p. 72.

pp. 208–11. **"A Letter to William Carlos Williams."** See *The Collected Shorter Poems of Kenneth Rexroth* (New York: New Directions, 1966), p. 193.

p. 212. Photograph of JL, *c.* 1994.

p. 213. Photograph of Williams, in the late 1940s, by John D. Schiff.

THE OLD BEAR: KENNETH REXROTH

Previously unpublished.

p. 215. **that summer when I drove down / from Alta.** If JL came to San Francisco from Alta, the year 1939 is likely, though the record of his first meeting with Rexroth is unclear and may have been earlier, perhaps in 1936. **An Autobiographical Novel.** The book was in fact first published by Doubleday in 1966 and then reissued in 1969 by ND, which subsequently brought out in 1991 a substantially revised and expanded edition, edited by Linda Hamalian.

p. 216. **the old house on Potrero Hill.** In the late 1930s, Rexroth and Marie Kass, soon to be his second wife, lived at 692 Wisconsin Street, on Potrero Hill in San Francisco.

pp. 218. **Right term for his fakeries / . . . / Was another inspiration.** There is evidently a page or more missing here. JL has shifted back in time to the period before Rexroth moved to Potrero Hill and was still living with his first wife, Andrée Schafer. **Eugene Debs, who went to / Jail for building up unions.** Debs was imprisoned in 1918–21 for opposing U.S. involvement in World War I.

TOM MERTON

Collected in *CR* and reprinted in *CAAS*.

p. 219. **Gethsemani, his monastery.** Thomas Merton, a convert to Catholicism, entered the Trappist monastery of Gethsemani in 1941, at the age of twenty-six. **Thirty Poems.** Published by ND in 1944. **PAX INTRANTIBUS.** Latin: "peace to those who enter."

p. 220. **lux in aeternitate.** Latin: "light in eternity."

pp. 222–23. **The Hammers . . . Hagia Sophia . . . Carolyn. . . .** Victor Hammer (1882–1967) was then teaching at Transylvania University in Lexington, KY, where he and his wife, Carolyn Reading Hammer, ran their press, the Stamperia del Santuccio, which published a number of small volumes by Merton, including an edition of his prose poem "Hagia Sophia" (1962). Later, in 1957, Carolyn Hammer was a founder the King Library Press at the University of Kentucky, Lexington, where she was the curator of rare books.

THE RUBBLE RAILROAD

Collected in *SR*. Previously published in *Ambit* 140 (1995) and *CAAS*.

p. 226. **I'd managed with / Some effort to avoid the war.** Although JL was classified 4F in 1940 because of his skiing injuries, he did contribute to the war effort, training U.S. troops in Utah to ski.

p. 233. **Mädels.** German: "girls."

p. 239. ***"Ungenügende Anlegung."*** German: "insufficient attention." ***"Grüss Gott / Herr."*** German: "Hello, sir." ***Schwimmbad.*** German: "swimming pool."

p. 241. ***"O Frères Humains."*** French: "O Brother Men."

THE WRONG BED—MOIRA

Collected in *CR* and *PNS*. First published in *Ambit* 133 (1993), with the following classical correlative and a marginal gloss that reads: "*Suggested by Catullus XXXI* [sic]"

(Part II) Ipsitilla

Ipsitilla, my sweet, dear girl,
Little furnace, send word at once,
Please, that I may spend the
Afternoon with you. And if I may,
Be sure no other cocks are let
Into your henhouse. And don't
You go walking the streets;
Stay home and have ready for me
Nine of your nicest continuous
Fucks. (And don't forget the
Wine.) May I come as soon as
Possible? I've had my lunch
But I'm hot for it and my
Prick is trying to poke holes
In my shirt and the blanket.

JL's colloquial rendering of Catullus XXXII was collected in *CR*.

THE YELLOW PAD

First published in *Ambit* 141 (1995) and reprinted in *CAAS*.
p. 245. **the magazine office.** International Publications. See p. 180.

THE DESERT IN BLOOM

Collected in *CR* and *PNS*. First published in *Ambit* 136 (1994)
and reprinted in *CAAS*. In *Ambit*, the poem was followed by a
classical correlative with the Latin title "Nox mihi candida" ("For
me bright night"), which JL gives to part VII of Pound's *Homage
to Sextus Propertius* (1917), acknowledged in a marginal gloss (see
Pound's *Personae*; ND, 1990). It concludes with a dedicatory note:
"This Section *for June* J.L."

Nox mihi candida

Me happy, night, night full of brightness;
Oh couch made happy by my long delectations;
How many words talked out with abundant candles;
Struggles when the lights were taken away;
Now with bared breasts she wrestled against me,
    Tunic spread in delay;
And she then opening my eyelids fallen in sleep,
Her lips upon them; and it was her mouth saying:
   Sluggard!

In how many varied embraces, our changing arms,
Her kisses, how many, lingering on my lips.
"Turn not Venus into a blinded motion,
    Eyes are the guides of love,
Paris took Helen naked coming from the bed of Menelaus,
Endymion's naked body, bright bait for Diana,"
    —such at least is the story.

While our fates twine together, sate we our eyes with love;
For long night comes upon you
        and a day when no day returns.
Let the gods lay chains upon us
    so that no day shall unbind them.

Fool who would set a term to love's madness,
For the sun shall drive with black horses,
    earth shall bring wheat from barley
The flood shall move toward the fountain
    Ere love know moderations,
    The fish shall swim in dry streams.
No, now while it may be, let not the fruit of life cease.

    Dry wreathes drop their petals,
      their stalks are woven in baskets,

To-day we take the great breath of lovers,
to-morrow fate shuts us in.

Though you give all your kisses
you give but few.

Nor can I shift my pains to other,
Hers will I be dead,
If she confer such nights upon me,
long is my life, long in years,
If she give me many,
God I am for the time.

p. 251. **You were George's sister, the / Beautiful poet's
beautiful sister.** The poem concerns June Oppen Degnan
(1918–2001), half-sister of the Objectivist poet George
Oppen (1908–84) and publisher of the *San Francisco Review*.
She and JL met around 1960. New Directions and San
Francisco Review Books copublished two of George Oppen's
books, *The Materials* (1962) and *This in Which* (1965), as well
as Charles Reznikoff's *By the Waters of Manhattan* (1962) and
Testimony: The United States 1885–1890 (1965).

pp. 251–52. *roucoulement des / Colombes.* French: "the cooing of
doves." *cansos.* Provençal: "canzones," or lyric songs.
Cassiopeia, whom Perseus saved. It was Andromeda, not
her mother Cassiopeia, whom Perseus rescued.

p. 253. *venerandam.* Latin: "to be adored" (i.e., sexually).

p. 254. **my third / Marriage.** Two years after the death of Ann
Laughlin in 1989, JL married Gertrude Huston, a former art director of ND and its principal book designer for most of the 1970s.

IN TRIVANDRUM

Collected in *SR* and *PNS*. First published in *CAAS* and reprinted in *Ambit* 145 (1996). Except for *Ambit*, the poem concludes

with the following endnote: "[*The author expresses his thanks to Hayden Carruth for his editorial collaboration on 'Trivandrum.'*]"

p. 255. **1953.** JL spent several weeks in India during the spring of that year, for his work with International Publications.

pp. 256–57. **Raja Rao. . . .*The Serpent and the Rope*. . . . *Kanthapura*. . . . New Directions brought / The book out at once.** JL's chronology is awkward here. Rao's *The Serpent and the Rope* wasn't published until 1960, while *Kanthapura*—his "new book"—came out in 1938 (London: Allen and Unwin), with the ND edition appearing in 1963.

MELISSA

First published in *Ambit* 135 (1994) and reprinted in *CAAS. Ambit* included the following classical correlative:

> Melissa—Part 2
> *Lines from the Amatory Epigrams of the Greek Anthology*

> (Very free adaptations from the translations of W.R. Paton)
> Melissa pulled one reddish hair
> From her braid and tied my hands
> With it. I was her prisoner. I   *Paulus Silentarius*
> Told her never to let me go.   (V, 230)

> Sometimes secret love affairs
> Yield more honey than those   *Paulus Silentarius*
> Which are open.   (V, 219)

> She kissed me one evening with
> Wet lips; her mouth smelt sweet
> As nectar. I'm drunk with her
> Kiss. I have drunk love in   *Anonymous*
> Abundance.   (V, 305)

Melissa's beauty is the gift of
The god Eros; Aphrodite charmed   *Meleager*
Her bed; the Graces gave her grace.   (V, 196)

In my heart Eros himself created
Sweet-voiced Melissa, the soul   *Meleager*
Of my soul.   (V, 154)

Might it not be that someday in
Legend soft-gliding Melissa will   *Meleager*
Surpass the Graces themselves?   (V, 148)

I swear, I swear it by Eros, I
Would rather hear her whisper in
My ear than listen to Apollo   *Meleager*
Playing on his lyre.   (V, 141)

I held her close, we were breast
To breast, hers supporting mine,
Her lips joined with mine. As for
The rest, the little bedlamp was the   *Marcus Argentarius*
Only witness; I am silent.   (V, 128)

Her kiss is like the lime that
Catches birds. Her eyes are fine
And when she looks at "me" I also burn.
If she touches me she has me caught   *Meleager*
Fast.   (V, 96)

I wish I were a rose, a pink rose,
For you to pick and press against   *Anonymous*
Your snowy breasts.   (V, 84)

Beauty without charm is only pleasing.
It's nothing to remember. It's like   *Capito*
Fishing with bait but no hook.   (V, 67)

We fell in love, we kissed, you gave
Yourself to me, we had much pleasure.
But who am I, and who are you? How
Did it happen that we came together?   *Anonymous*
Only the Kyprian goddess knows.   (V, 51)

Gray are her lovely eyes, her cheeks
Of crystal. Could you not call her
Sweet mouth a rose? Her neck is of
Marble, breasts smooth as marble.
Her small feet? They are more charming   *Rufinus*
Than those of silver-footed Thetis.   (V, 48)

For so long, my darling, I prayed to
Have you with me at night, touching
And caressing. And now your love has
Brought me that happiness. You are
Beside me, naked. But why do I become   *Rufinus*
Drowsy? I owe you this felicity forever.   (V, 47)

Beware a girl who is too ready,
But also one who hangs back too
Long. One is too quick, the other
Too slow. Look for one who is
Neither too plump nor too thin.
Too little flesh is as bad as too   *Rufinus*
Much. Never run to excess.   (V, 42 & 37)

Whether you have colored your hair
Dark or have it its natural shade,
It *frames* your dear face in beauty.
The god Eros loves your hair and
Will still be twining his fingers   *Anonymous*
In it when it is gray.   (V, 26)

Shall we take a shower together,
Soaping ourselves and rubbing each
Other, flesh to flesh; then put on

Our robes and sip a good wine? The
Season of such joys is short; then   *Rufinus*
Comes old age and finally death.   (V, 12)

Make the bedlamp tipsy with oil;
It's the silent confidant of things
We seldom dare to speak of. Then
Let it go out. There are times when
The god Eros wants no living witness.
Close the door tight. Then let the
Bed, the lovers' friend, teach us   *Philodemus*
The rest of Aphrodite's secrets.   (V, 4)

p. 271. **Melissa.** I.e., the British artist Vanessa Jackson, whom JL met in London in 1981.

BROWN

Previously unpublished.

p. 276. **Brown.** In the spring of 1983, JL taught a one-semester course at Brown University in Providence, RI.

EPILOGUE: A HONEST HEART . . . A KNOWING HEAD

First published in *PNS*.

p. 278. *a letter to Peter Carr.* JL extracts passages from Thomas Jefferson's letter of August 17, 1785, written from Paris, to his nephew Peter Carr. For the complete text, see *The Life and Selected Writings of Thomas Jefferson*, edited by Adrienne Koch and William Peden (New York: The Modern Library, 1944), pp. 373–77.

ACKNOWLEDGMENTS

Many people had a part in bringing this book into existence. I am especially grateful to the Trustees of the New Directions Ownership Trust (Daniel Javitch, chair, Peggy L. Fox, Donald S. Lamm, and Griselda Ohannessian), which holds the copyrights to James Laughlin's work, for inviting me to edit *Byways*. I would like to thank in addition Daniel Javitch and Leila Laughlin Javitch, for gathering JL's manuscripts and valuable Laughlin family photographs; Ian MacNiven, JL's biographer, for his generous sharing of research; Michele Lowrie, Richard Sieburth, Burton Pike, and Minna Proctor, for their linguistic expertise; Dr. Joanna Chapin and Roger and Liddie Christenfeld, for their memories of JL; my New Directions colleagues Kurt Beals, Peggy Fox, Thomas Keith, Sylvia Frezzolini Severance, Jeffrey Young, and most especially Barbara Epler, for their thousand helps and professional support; my wife, Suzanne Thibodeau, for her sure editor's eye—and above all, JL himself: it was an honor to have done this book for him.   —PG

Some of the poems in this book were first published, often in substantially different form, in *Ambit* (London) and *Contemporary Authors Autobiographical Series*, vol. 22 (Detroit, MI: Gale Research, Inc., 1996). Others were originally collected in James Laughlin's *The Country Road* (Cambridge, MA: Zoland Books, 1995) and *The Secret Room* (New Directions, 1997), as well as in his posthumous *Poems New and Selected* (New Directions, 1998).

Remembering William Carlos Williams was originally published separately as a New Directions Paperbook Original in 1994. Grateful acknowledgment is made to New Directions Publishing

321

Photographs and picture credits; all Williams family photographs of William Carlos Williams and others (p. 143; p. 171—Raquel Hélène Rose Hoheb Williams; p. 189—9 Ridge Road, Rutherford, NJ; p. 190—William Carlos Williams and Florence H. Williams; p. 202) courtesy of the Estate of William Eric Williams and the Estate of Paul H. Williams; all book jackets courtesy of the New Directions archives; all nonfamily photographs of William Carlos Williams are from New Directions files and are here identified by photographer (p. 142, Charles Sheeler; p. 169, Eve Arnold; p. 181, Irving Wellcome; p. 191, Tram; p. 195, James Laughlin; p. 213, John D. Schiff); the drawing of William Carlos Williams on p. 183 by Ben Shahn; the photograph of James Laughlin on p. 147 by Poley Storey and the photograph of James Laughlin on p. 212, from the Laughlin family photographs, courtesy of Daniel Javitch and Leila Laughlin Javitch; the drawing of the Passaic Falls, by Earl Horter, courtesy of the State Library of New Jersey.

General photograph credits: cover photograph of James Laughlin by Man Ray, courtesy of Daniel Javitch and Leila Laughlin Javitch; frontispiece, James Laughlin, by Virginia Schendler, used by permission; all Laughlin family photographs (p. 10—James Laughlin's great-grandfather; p. 11—James Laughlin's grandfather; p. 15—James Laughlin; p. 19—Sidney Page Laughlin and James Laughlin; p. 30—Henry Hughart Laughlin, by Strickler; p. 68, Margery Rea Laughlin, by Bachrach; p. 135, Leila Laughlin Carlisle; p. 139, Laughlin family wedding) courtesy of Daniel Javitch and Leila Laughlin Javitch.